Moray & Badenoch

Moray & Badenoch

A Historical Guide

Richard Oram

First published in Great Britain, 1996,
by Birlinn Ltd,
14 High Street,
Edinburgh EH1 1TE

British Library Cataloguing-in-Publication Data
A Catalogue record for this book is available from the British Library.

ISBN 1 874744 46 7

Typeset in Plantin Light

Printed and bound in Finland by W.S.O.Y.

ACKNOWLEDGEMENTS

I owe a great number of debts to a great many people, accrued during the preparation of this book. To my wife, Justine, must go my greatest thanks for her fortitude in bearing up as I dragged her to yet another 'pile of rubble' on a wind- and rain-swept moor, and for her tolerance in permitting me to disappear for hours on end to huddle over my word-processor. A similar debt is owed to my son, Alasdair, who visited his first Ancient Monument at four weeks old, and who, in his own inimitable way was always there to tell me when enough was enough.

My especial thanks are due to Jim Inglis of the Elgin Museum, Janet Trythall and Susan Bennett, without whose unstinting generosity in providing information and advice this book would have been very much the poorer; to Ian Keillar, whose enthusiasm and encyclopaedic knowledge of Moray made me rethink my ideas on some matters; and to Geoff Stell of the Royal Commission on the Ancient and Historical Monuments of Scotland, for his freely given advice and encouragement. My final thanks must go to Hugh Andrew of Birlinn Ltd., whose own interest in Scottish history and archaeology provided the spur for this book's genesis.

CONTENTS

FIGURES

MAPS

PLATES

PREFACE

Together, Moray and Badenoch constitute a slice through the landscape character of Scotland. Along the 110-mile course of the Spey, which runs like a life-giving artery through the countryside, the traveller passes from the bleak wastes of the central Highlands, through the forests of Strathspey, to the douce lowlands which fringe the inner reaches of the Moray Firth. At the southern end of the region are the deep, glaciated valleys which burst out from the sub-arctic country of the Cairngorm and Monadhliath plateaux, much of which rises to in excess of 1100m. Here are expanses of blanket bog and heather moorland, much of it still free from modern forestry plantation. The river valleys, though broad, are marshy-bottomed or, where drained, covered by poor and stoney soils with only a narrow band of better ground on the lower slopes at their margins. Between Kingussie and Aviemore, Strathspey opens out into a wide, relatively flat-bottomed valley, its surface punctuated by a string of kettle-lake lochs (e.g. Loch Insh and Loch Alvie), and watery flats prone to winter flooding. Agriculturalists have scraped an existence on the lower slopes here for over 5000 years, but large parts of the valley bottom are now given over to forestry plantations. Beyond Nethy Bridge the valley narrows and is hemmed in to east and west by the southern Morayshire hills. North of Grantown-on-Spey, in the bleak moors around Dava and Lochindorb, these rise to over 400m, broken on their northern rim by the deep gorges of the rivers Divie and Findhorn. This is still a Highland landscape of hill-farms, grouse moor and forestry, where winter often lingers late on the north-facing hillsides, but it gives way in a space of less than two miles to the broad lowland of the Laich of Moray. It is a sharp divide and, until the later 19th century, it was a cultural as well as a geographical boundary which separated the Gaelic-speaking parishes of the highland zone from the English-speaking country of the Laich. This is a rolling countryside of arable fields, warmer and drier than the southern hills, and here, too, is located the bulk of the population of the region. Here the Highland rivers Spey and Findhorn break out from the confines of their valley and gorge to spill over the sandy plain to the Moray Firth.

At no time since the Reformation have the regions covered within this book formed part of a larger jurisdictional whole, be it secular or ecclesiastic. The boundaries of the area covered are formed by those of pre-1974 Morayshire (therefore excluding that large part of north-west Banffshire which has been incorporated into its two post-1974 successor authorities), and by the medieval deanery of Strathspey (chosen in preference to Badenoch and Strathspey District). There will, no doubt, be complaints about the rigid adherence to the boundaries selected, for some sites which lie literally yards across the frontier (such as the standing stone at Melgarve on the north side of the Spey in the upper reaches of the river valley, which lies in Badenoch and Strathspey District, but was in the medieval deanery of Inverness) have been omitted. A line, however, had to be drawn somewhere.

It is advisable for anyone visiting the sites listed in this book to use Ordnance Survey maps. By far the best maps are the Pathfinder Series (1:25000 scale), but most sites are marked on the Landranger Series (1:50000 scale), of which only five sheets (Nos 27, 28, 35, 36 and 42) are needed to cover the whole region.

The sites listed in this book represent a wide, but far from exhaustive, selection of the many monuments in this archaeologically and historically rich region. In general, greater detail has been given to the pre-1600 sections, with most sites which are marked on the 1:50000 Landranger Series Ordnance Survey maps being included. The greater selectivity in the post-1600 period has a variety of determining reasons behind it. In part it reflects the proliferation of surviving buildings from this era. For example, most post-1800 mansions are omitted except where an earlier structure lies at their core, and those in the 1700–1800 period are intended to offer only a representative sample to avoid creating an imbalance. Similar reasons govern the selection of monuments in the various categories of bridges, communication and transport. The relative poverty of sites in the agricultural settlement category, however, is a reflection of the limited amount of work yet undertaken in the upland districts of both Moray and Badenoch and is a clear indication of the need for such work.

It is essential to bear in mind that many of these sites are on private ground and inclusion in this book should not be taken as an automatic guarantee of any right of access. Only those marked with an asterisk (*) are in guardianship of the Secretary of State for Scotland, most being subject to standard Historic Scotland opening times and regulations. In most other cases, permission should be sought from the nearest farm, house, forestry or estate office before setting out across country.

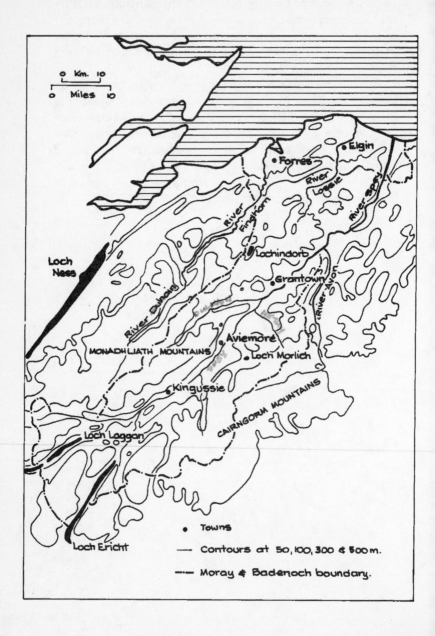

Km. 10

Miles 10

Elgin

Forres

River Lossie

River Findhorn

River Spey

Loch Ness

Lochindorb

Grantown

River Dulnain

River Avon

Aviemore

MONADHLIATH MOUNTAINS

Loch Morlich

Kingussie

CAIRNGORM MOUNTAINS

Loch Laggan

Loch Ericht

• Towns

—— Contours at 50, 100, 300 & 500 m.

—·—· Moray & Badenoch boundary.

INTRODUCTION

PALAEOLITHIC PERIOD

Before *c.*7000 BC

On the summit plateau of Creag Meagaidh in western Badenoch in late winter, when the bitter east wind is blowing across the icy tops, it is not difficult to envisage the conditions which gripped northern Scotland during the more extreme phases of the last Ice Age. From about 25,000 BC down to about 13,000 BC much of the land was mantled under a thick covering of ice, or at best was a treeless tundra akin to present-day Canada or Siberia north of the tree-line. After 13,000 BC the climate began to improve and the ice-sheet retreated, until by about 10,000 BC only parts of the northern and western Highlands were under ice and a few glaciers lingered in the northern corries of the Cairngorms. There were times in the period down to 8300 BC when the ice advanced again, but gradually the sub-arctic wastes were to give way to dense forests of birch and pine.

It is usually said that there was no human settlement possible under such extreme conditions in the region which became Scotland, but the ice cover was never wholly complete nor was it permanent for the whole of the Ice Age, and occasional hunting parties may have made their way north. This was the so-called Palaeolithic (Old Stone Age) era, when the first humans of 'modern' type (Homo sapiens sapiens) began to cross the land bridges which still connected Britain with northern Europe to occupy the hunting lands around the limits of the ice. Evidence for human activity, however, is limited largely to areas of southern England and Wales which lay on the margins of the ice-sheet or beyond its southernmost reach. For most of the rest of Britain, its landscape repeatedly scoured by the ice, or buried beneath a deep layer of boulder clay, any such evidence has either been lost forever or concealed beneath a deep overburden.

MESOLITHIC PERIOD

c.7000 BC to c.4000 BC

As the climate warmed and the ice retreated, wandering bands of what are referred to as 'hunters and gatherers', living a lifestyle very similar to that of the North American Plains Indians before the arrival of European colonists in the 19th century, began to move into the northern parts of Britain. These people used different types of tools and weapons from the Palaeolithic people who preceded them and are labelled Mesolithic, or Middle Stone Age. They lived a simple life, exploiting the natural resources of the land, hunting the abundant game and wildfowl, fishing in inland and coastal waters, gathering nuts, berries and other edible plants. They shaped stone, mainly flints, for weapons and tools, dressed in the skins of the animals which they hunted, and lived a nomadic lifestyle, moving with the seasons and in pursuit of better hunting.

We do not know the routes which they followed into the north, but it is likely that they came a variety of ways: by sea into the Hebrides, from southern England, or across the wide plain now occupied by the North Sea. The earliest Mesolithic settlement yet excavated in Scotland, at Loch Scresort in Rum, is almost 9000 years old, but it is unlikely to be the *oldest* settlement site in Scotland as the land had been suitable for habitation up to 1000 years earlier. By about 8000 years ago there were Mesolithic encampments in the coastal area around Oban, on Arran, and on the Hebridean islands of Islay, Jura and Ulva, while a site discovered in Inverness has been dated only slightly later. Encampments in Fife and up the east coast into Aberdeenshire have been dated to c.6000 BC.

The occupation sites of this period are often betrayed by a scatter of tiny flint flakes on the ground surface, exposed by ploughing or erosion, or by irregularly shaped mounds of debris, mainly sea-shells, the remains of refuse middens. There are no structural remains as such; their shelters were lightweight and have left little more than traces of stake-holes in the soil. Most of the sites yet discovered are located near to the sea or in the lower reaches of important river valleys, sited to make the best use of the natural food resources.

In the country between the site at Inverness and those at Newburgh, Banchory and Nethermills around Aberdeen, no Mesolithic site has been identified positively, but stray finds of characteristic flints from the Culbin Sands and possible shell-middens in the area east of Lossiemouth suggest that these early hunters were not avoiding the lagoons, marshes and coast of the Laich of Moray. It is likely, too, that the broad strath of the Spey, pushing deep inland from the Moray coast, will yet produce evidence of Mesolithic people.

Mesolithic Sites

1. Caysbriggs, Lossiemouth
NJ 245 675

This possible group of shell-middens lies in forestry 2.5 miles south-east of Lossiemouth, c.100m north of the Caysbriggs ringwork (see below), immediately to the east of the track from Caysbriggs. One area is eroding out of the steep embankment of a gravel terrace overlooking the eastern limits of the drained bed of Spynie Loch, with a further two rabbit-burrowed mounds set on the level summit of the terrace.

2. Culbin Sands, Forres
[Un-referenced]

Stray finds of flints and flint flakes have been recovered at various times over the last 100 or so years from several locations within the now forest-covered area of coastal sand dunes between Forres and Nairn.

3. Romancamp Gate, Fochabers
NJ 356 617

Excavation of an Iron Age settlement which survived as a series of crop-marks on the edge of the 25m terrace above the east side of the Spey estuary (see below p.47) uncovered evidence that the area had been previously settled in the Mesolithic. Evidence in the form of a scatter of flints (tools and flakes), suggested that the Iron Age site overlay the edge of a Mesolithic flint-knapping site, the centre of which was not located in the course of the excavation.

4.   **Spynie, Elgin**
     NJ 228 659
Exploratory excavation along the shoreline of the drained Spynie Loch, immediately west of the medieval bishops' palace, aimed at examination of the possible harbour and 'fisher toun', revealed evidence instead for an important prehistoric occupation of the site. Large pits, filled with shells, indicated the presence of a settlement by the loch, or tidal inlet as it would then have been, dating from late Mesolithic or early Neolithic times.

NEOLITHIC

c.4000 BC to *c*.2500 BC

From around about 6000 years ago, new peoples began to cross from north-west Europe into Britain, bringing with them new ideas and new technologies. Their way of life was markedly different from that of the nomadic Mesolithic hunter-gatherers, for it was based on a settled existence in communities which supported themselves by agriculture, growing cereal crops (primitive varieties of wheat and barley) and rearing cattle and sheep. They used new types of tools and weapons, still of stone and flint, but fashioned in different ways from those of the Mesolithic people, and they knew how to make pottery. To this new culture, archaeologists apply the label Neolithic (New Stone Age), and with it we enter a world where for the first time we can see the physical evidence for their activities in standing monuments in the landscape.

The movement of Neolithic people into Britain came from a number of directions: from the south across the Channel and up through England; by sea from Ireland into western Scotland, the Hebrides and the Northern Isles; and across the North Sea into the eastern seaboard. They were moving into a landscape which was still largely cloaked in dense forest, virgin territory the preserve previously of only wandering bands of hunters. There was no overnight transformation – the Mesolithic people did not simply settle down and turn into farmers – and it is likely that the two cultures co-existed for perhaps several centuries before the Neolithic way of life gradually absorbed the earlier groups. In any case, the clearance of the forest to make way for fields, and the constant need to expand the area of cultivation as the soil became exhausted under the primitive agriculture which knew nothing of crop rotation, was incompatible with the earlier tradition. Free-roaming hunters and settled farmers lived in different worlds.

One of the biggest differences between the Mesolithic and Neolithic peoples was the settled existence of the latter and

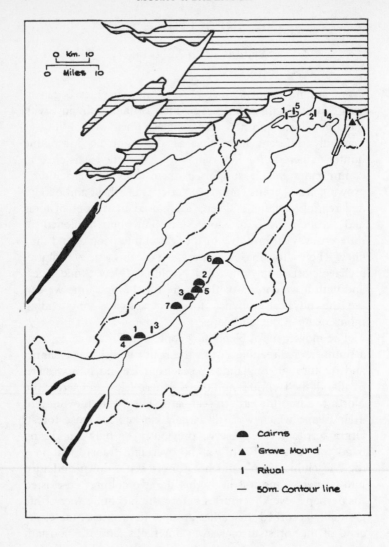

1. Neolithic – cairns, grave mounds and ritual sites

the development of communities to which the term society could truly be attached. Cereal cultivation, stock-rearing and the exploitation of the natural resources through hunting and fishing, allowed the growth of larger settlements. Few of the earliest Neolithic settlement sites in Scotland have been identified, let alone excavated, and most of our knowledge of these people comes from the communal tombs which they built. One of the earliest settlements identified and excavated is at Balbridie on Deeside, where a great timber-built hall 24.5m long by 13m wide formed the focus for the farming community. Further north, in Orkney and Shetland, stone-built houses at sites such as Knap of Howar and Skara Brae give a unique insight into the life of these first farmers, with stone furnishings such as box-beds and 'dressers' for storage and the display of pottery, tools and utensils of stone and bone, and the debris of their food preserved in the middens and under the sand which engulfed the settlements. Numerous finds of pottery and fine polished stone axes from the Laich of Moray (e.g. at Kennieshillock NJ 302 607, Wallfield NJ 294 652, Longhill NJ 274 627, or Meft NJ 268 639) demonstrate that the light sandy soils of that area supported one of the two major areas of Neolithic settlement in north-east Scotland (the other is in the Garioch in central Aberdeenshire), but few settlement sites have been positively identified in this zone. Evidence for what appears to have been a flint-working site in the vicinity of Lochindorb shows that the upland districts were as attractive to the early agriculturalists.

Excavations in the 19th century at a now unlocated site at Roseisle in the Laich of Moray uncovered what appears to have been both a ritual and settlement site, but the report of the work is almost incomprehensible. In view of the later importance of this same area in the Bronze and Iron Ages, and in the early Middle Ages, however, it seems likely that it formed a focus for settlement in the Neolithic, too. Traces of Neolithic activity were located during excavations near the medieval bishop's palace at Spynie. At *Bellie*, excavation of the grave-mound produced evidence for the presence of a Neolithic community in the immediate vicinity, although the settlement site itself lay beyond the limits of the excavated area.

Where there are no surviving remains of settlement above ground, the burial places of these early farmers often still stand boldly on the sky-line to mark their passing. Strangely, too, there is a near absence of burial sites of forms readily identified as Neolithic from most of Moray, the small burial mound excavated near Fochabers in the 1970s possibly representing a local funerary tradition. Indeed, Moray is something of a blank zone between the large and complex long cairns of Banffshire and Aberdeenshire and the so-called Clava-type cairns (named after the site at Clava near Inverness) and related ring-cairns found in Nairnshire, around the upper end of the Great Glen, and in a dense cluster around the middle reaches of the Spey in Badenoch. The Clava cairns are the most striking of the Neolithic monuments which survive in Moray and Badenoch and are impressive testimony to the collective effort which built them as communal tombs of the ancestors in the 3rd millennium BC. They consist of circular stone cairns contained within a kerb of massive boulders, the largest placed on the south-west. The cairn is contained within a stone circle, the stones of which are graded in height, again with the highest towards the south-west. There are two forms of such tomb, the passage graves where the central chamber is reached down a short passage from an entrance in the south-west side of the cairn, and ring cairns, where the chamber was infilled after the burials were in place and the superstructure of the cairn built over it. None of these cairns has been excavated in its entirety using modern methods, and most which have been examined have been disturbed at some time in the past.

The finest of these cairns in the area covered by this book lie in the district around Aviemore, and are believed to have been built as collective tombs by colonists who moved out of the core area of Clava settlement in the area around the head of the Moray Firth into the broad upper strath of the Spey. The Historic Scotland maintained site at *Aviemore* has lost most of its cairn superstructure and only the kerb and part of the enclosing stone circle survive, but it conveys a good impression of the key features which lie at the heart of the often amorphous piles of stone which many have become. The best-preserved of the cairns are at *Avielochan*, excavated in 1909 and with its passage and chamber left open, and *Granish*, where the massive kerb of granite boulders offers silent testimony to the engineering skills and physical efforts of its Neolithic builders. The site at *Glenbanchor* appears to represent an isolated example of a different funerary tradition found more usually east of the Spey in Banffshire and Buchan, the long cairn, where the superstructure extends in an elongated tail from the burial chamber, but this identification has yet to be confirmed. Similar doubts must be cast on the identification of the badly-disturbed site of Bank of Roseisle (NJ 149 670).

Along with the burial monuments, ritual sites form the most impressive memorials to the Neolithic peoples. Again, Moray has a striking dearth of such sites, despite the evidence which shows it to have been an important centre of population. The main types of structure are stone circles and henges, and these can be found clustered densely in Aberdeenshire, especially in the Garioch, and in the lands around the head of the Moray Firth. Although it is usually said that there are no henges – earthwork sites where a ceremonial area, often a stone circle or ring of timber posts, occupies a central platform reached by one causeway (Class I) or two or more (Class II), enclosed by a deep ditch with the upcast mound of excavated material on the *outer* side – between Wormiehillock near Rhynie and Dingwall in Easter Ross, the enigmatic earthwork at *Quarrywood* has henge-like features. Such monuments are usually dated between *c.*2500 and 2000 BC.

Neolithic Sites

Cairns:

1. Altlarie, Tom a' Chladha, Newtonmore
NN 726 995

This cairn, apparently of Clava type, sits on a small mound (Tom a' Chladha) on the rising ground above the Spey at the north-east end of Newtonmore, immediately to the west of the railway track. The kerbstones, which scarcely show through the turf, enclose a cairn 15m in diameter and rising no more than 1m in height.

2. Avielochan, Aviemore
NH 908 167

This Clava passage-grave, excavated in 1909, lies on the floor of Strathspey, occupying a small mound at the edge of a field immediately west of the railway line, reached down an access track from Avielochan. The kerb, of irregular boulders, has been disturbed in places but encloses an area of *c.*12.6m. Most of its inner face has been exposed by removal of the cairn structure, but near the central chamber in excess of 1.25m in depth of cairn material survives. The bank which encloses the cairn, most prominent to the east and north, is probably composed of field dump and stones from the interior of the kerb.

The chamber and passage were left exposed after the excavation. The latter is 4.4m long and runs in from the south towards

Figure 1. Avielochan, Clava-type cairn

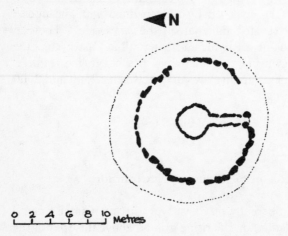

the chamber, which may have been constructed in a natural hollow as the passage appears to run downhill into it. The outer end is built of boulders, the inner of split slabs, the whole rising to a maximum height of 0.8m. The passage is 0.68m wide at its outer end and 0.89 where it enters the chamber.

The chamber is subcircular with a diameter of c.3.2m. Its wall rises to a maximum of 0.68m, its lowest courses made up of boulders and slabs set on their long sides, with a few courses of flattish slabs above. Some traces of paving in the north-west of the chamber were found during excavation.

The denuded remains of a smaller second cairn lie 11m to the south-west. It is 7.5m in diameter and a few kerbstones are visible through the turf.

3. Aviemore*
NH 896 134

This ruined ring cairn of Clava type is situated in a housing estate towards the north end of the town. The cairn material has been removed, leaving the near-complete kerb exposed. This encloses an area 13.25m in diameter. The outer faces of the kerbstones are flat, touching at the ends to present a smooth face, while the inner faces are very irregular. The tallest stones (rising to 1m) are in the south-west segment of the ring. The space between the kerb and the inner setting is very narrow (2.8m), forming a very large chamber (c.7.5m diameter).

The cairn was originally enclosed by a stone circle. In 1877 seven stones survived, of which only four remain.

4. Glenbanchor, Newtonmore
NN 678 994

Identified as a long cairn, this prominent site lies aligned north-south on the broad alluvial terrace of the River Calder, north-west of Glenballoch farm. It is a regular mound 30m long, 11m wide at the north end and 12.6m at the south, rising to 1.6m in height. The ends show no signs of curved façades, but this may be a consequence of past ploughing right up to its base. There are no traces of kerbs or chambers.

5.   Granish, (Loch na Carraigean), Aviemore
NH 907 154

This ring-cairn lies on the east side of the railway, between the rail-track and the path, just south of marshy Loch na Carraigean 2m north-north-east of Aviemore. To the west lie many small cairns, possibly field-clearance mounds of the Bronze Age or later.

Granish is one of the most impressive monuments of this type in Badenoch. The kerb is virtually complete and encloses an area 17.6m in diameter. Composed of granite blocks with flat outer surfaces and irregular inner faces, it is graded in height towards the south-west where the stones rise

Figure 2. Granish, ring cairn

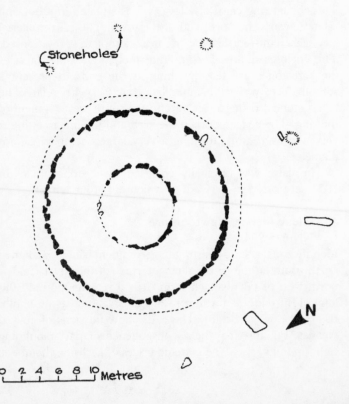

to 1.1m in height. There is a slight bank of stony material set against the outer face of the kerb.

The internal setting is 7.5m in diameter, set 10.1m inside the outer kerb, and is carefully constructed to give a smooth inner face. The stones are again graded in height towards the south-west. The cairn structure, composed of rounded alluvial pebbles, still rises flush with the tops of the outer kerb and inner setting. There was originally an outer circle of standing stones around the cairn, three fallen stones remaining.

6. Lackgie, (Tullochgorum)
NH 963 213

This Clava-type cairn stands on a knoll in the undulating agricultural land on the gravel terrace of the Spey on the south side of the A95 between Lackgie and Tullochgorum farms. Heavily robbed, little of the cairn structure survives but the kerb remains virtually complete and encloses an area of *c.*14m. Constructed of irregular rounded boulders, there are some suggestions of height grading towards the south and west. A bank of cairn material survives outside the kerb, but within it the inner ring has been reduced to a fragmentary setting of five earth-fast boulders. The stump of one stone and a fallen monolith, placed 5m outside the kerb, suggest the former presence of an enclosing stone circle.

7. Wester Delfour
NH 844 086

This ring-cairn lies in agricultural land on the west side of Strathspey, immediately to the north of Wester Delfour farm. Recorded as being subject to the dumping of field stones in the early part of this century, by the late 1950s these had been cleared – and with them most of the cairn structure. The kerb survives almost complete, built of large blocks which are graded in height towards the south-west (1.3m max.), enclosing an area *c.*18.3m in diameter.

The carefully built inner ring of stones is almost complete and is constructed of similarly graded blocks to the outer kerb. Placed 5.36m inside the outer kerb, it encloses a subcircular area *c.*6.6m in diameter.

To the south-south-west of the cairn, 7.1m from the kerb, is a single impressive monolith 3m high. A slab of similar scale lies fallen against the low bank which encircles the kerb – itself probably an original feature – indicating that there was perhaps originally a full circle of such stones around the cairn.

Grave Mounds

1.   Bellie, Fochabers
NJ 359 592

This important site stood at Boghead in the Speymouth Forest, 800m north of the A98 Fochabers to Buckie road. Excavation following the destruction of one half of the mound during the construction of a new track by the Forestry Commission in 1971 revealed this to be a highly complex site dating from the earlier 4th millennium BC, re-used in the late Neolithic, the Bronze Age, and possibly the Iron Age.

Before the bulldozer damage, the mound had been circular, roughly 15m in diameter, and consisted of sand covering a core of stones and boulders which possibly represented the remains of a cairn or cairns. Dug into the top of the mound were a series of eight inhumation burials (further burials may have been destroyed before excavation). The skeletal remains, where they had not been disturbed, were well preserved and most of the burials could be aged and sexed approximately as six male and one female, ranging in age from adolescence to c.40. There was no firm dating evidence for these graves, but their position in the mound indicates that they were probably Iron Age.

Adjacent to the burials was a small stone cist. This contained the poorly cremated remains of a young female and an infant. Positive dating was again impossible, but analogy indicates that this was a Bronze Age multiple cremation, the first of its kind from Moray.

Next in the chronology of use of the mound was a small pit which contained the remains of Beaker pottery. This was dated to c.2600 BC. The pottery was of a type associated with cooking and storage vessels rather than ritual or burials, and it is suggested that a wandering group of late Neolithic people had settled for a while in the vicinity of the mound.

The earliest activity on the site dates from shortly before 3750 BC. Soil and pollen analysis of the old ground surface beneath the mound showed that there had been limited early agriculture in the vicinity, making it one of the earliest known agricultural sites in Scotland. Charcoal remains from the soil indicated that the ground on which the mound was later constructed had been cleared by slash-and-burn techniques, and pollen showed that mixed crops of six-row barley and emmer-wheat had been grown. The attendant settlement had been largely obliterated by the building of the burial mound, but survived as scatters of flint flakes, pot-sherds, stake holes for wind-breaks and patches of burning which may represent residual traces of fires.

It is not clear how long occupation of the site lasted, but its end was marked by a major fire on the summit of a natural knoll in the centre of the area, probably a funeral pyre. A cairn had then been built over the site of the pyre. Around it was a spread of dirty soil containing midden material and many pot-sherds, on which had then been constructed a series of small stone cairns.

Ritual

1. **Alves**
    NJ 162 628
This small circle, approximately seven metres in diameter, is unmarked on the 1:50000 OS map. Standing in woodland at about the 50m contour on the southern slopes of the Knock of Alves, 200m south of the hillfort, it consists of six earthfast boulders – one fallen – with a single outlying stone 7m to the west.

2. **Kingussie**
    c.NH 761 001 (lost)
When the parish church at the eastern end of the town was reconstructed in 1792, the 'standing stones of Easter Kingussie' which stood near the site were, according to local tradition, swept away. The site is of particular importance, as

it appears to have been used in the Middle Ages as the meeting-place of the head court of the lordship of Badenoch. It was at the stones on 10 October 1380 that Alexander Stewart, the Wolf of Badenoch, convened his court to settle his dispute over land in Badenoch with Alexander Bur, bishop of Moray.

3.   Lochhill, (The Deil's Stanes or The Nine Stanes), Urquhart
NJ 289 641

The remaining five stones of this circle stand in the corner of a field on the west of the unclassified Urquhart to Lochhill road, immediately north of the crossroads with the unclassified Lossiemouth to Garmouth road. The circle stands on sloping ground on the edge of a long ridge overlooking the Innes estate. Originally 36.6m in diameter, the interior of the circle has been used as a dump for field stones and the south-western arc has been ploughed into. The surviving stones, irregular earth-fast pillars of pink granite and grey sandstone, are located four to the south and east and one isolated on the north-west. The tallest stone, at the south, stands 1.83m high. The apparent grading of the stones and the tradition that there was an "altar" has led to suggestions that this was a recumbent circle of the type found most commonly in Aberdeenshire. If so, it is a remote western outlier of that tradition.

4.   Quarry Wood, Elgin
NJ 185 631

In a clearing in the forestry slightly to the south-east of the summit of Quarry Wood Hill, c.1 mile west of Elgin. Occupying a gently sloping terrace above the steeper ground on the south and south-east faces of the hill, this site would formerly have enjoyed dramatic views over the Lossie valley. Marked on the OS 1:50000 series map as a 'henge', but not currently accepted as such, it consists of a roughly circular platform 47m by 43m, sloping slightly towards the south-west. It is enclosed by a now heavily silted segmental ditch up to 5m wide and between 1m and 1.5m deep, beyond which are the remains of a bank formed by the upcast material from the ditch. Three pillar stones from a stone circle, the largest *c.*1m high, survive at the outer edge of the south-west quadrant of the platform, the northernmost broken in two pieces. The western sector of the ditch and bank show signs of considerable disturbance, but there are traces of a causeway across the ditch at this point.

THE BRONZE AGE

*c.*2500 BC to *c.*700 BC

Some 4500 years ago, a technological revolution occurred which transformed the nature of prehistoric culture in Britain. Migrants from the lands around the mouth of the Rhine crossed the North Sea to the British east coast and began to settle. There is an archaeological debate at present as to whether this migration was a major invasion, or that the new people arrived in small numbers and sought quickly to integrate with the existing communities, but the weight of evidence seems to point to the former. The newcomers formed a distinctive group among the earlier Neolithic people, physically, culturally and, above all, technologically. With them they brought new styles of pottery, notably the vessels which give them the name by which they are usually known: the Beaker People. But their one skill which set them apart from the Neolithic farmers was the knowledge of how to work in metal.

The discovery of metal-working technology was one of the great revolutions of prehistory and marked a time of profound change in the structures of society. It has been pointed out that this was not merely the substitution of stone and flint by a superior material, for metallurgy involved the acquisition of new skills, such as identification of ore-bearing rocks, smelting of ores, alloying metals and casting. Such skills are likely to have been jealously guarded and gave power and prestige to those who possessed them over those who did not. Possession of the raw materials necessary for the making of bronze gave a different form of power: economic. Copper and even more so tin ores are not evenly distributed within Britain, so demand for the new metal by people in areas which lacked natural deposits of metal ores stimulated trade, giving power to those who controlled the supply. Although copper is found in various locations around Scotland, none is a major source and most was imported into the north via long trade routes through the Highland valleys, but all tin had to be imported from Cornwall.

Long distance contacts, such as the Cornish tin trade, were

developed and maintained throughout the Bronze Age. There is some evidence to suggest that in the early 1st millennium BC – *c.*700 BC – there was either close trading links between the southern coastal area of the Moray Firth and north-west Germany, or settlement of peoples from Germany in this part of Scotland. The strongest evidence for this is in the form of fine bronze brooches of a distinctively German form found in the excavations at *Sculptor's Cave*, Covesea, and other ornamental bronze-work from sites in Aberdeenshire and Angus.

In north-eastern Scotland it appears that the Beaker People moved into areas between the major centres of Neolithic culture in the Garioch and the Laich of Moray. The Deveron Valley in Banffshire, for example, became an early and important centre of metal-working, but two stone moulds for bronze axes of early Bronze Age type have been recovered from the Culbin Sands. The nature of the incomers' relationship with the existing Neolithic communities can only be guessed at, but evidence for the 'slighting' or perhaps ritual desecration of earlier tombs and ceremonial sites hints at a not altogether harmonious encounter. We should not, however, doubt the power of the incomers and such acts as the burial of beakers at henges and recumbent circles should perhaps be seen as a statement of the superior 'magic' of the metal-workers. It is possible that the possessors of the new skills came to form an elite element in society, perhaps using the demand for their product amongst the Neolithic farmers to establish themselves in a ruling position over their 'customers'. Certainly, it is clear that the emerging Bronze Age society was a radically different one from what had gone before, with the development of a hierarchical structure with clear ruling classes, warrior castes and probably slavery.

The transformation of society is seen most clearly in the type of burial practice which evolved. The communal tombs of the Neolithic appear already to have been passing into disuse towards the close of the 3rd millennium BC, but they disappear altogether in the Bronze Age. Instead, individual burials in stone-lined box-graves – cists – became the norm. Some were inserted at first into the sides of earlier Neolithic cairns, for example at several of the major burial sites around

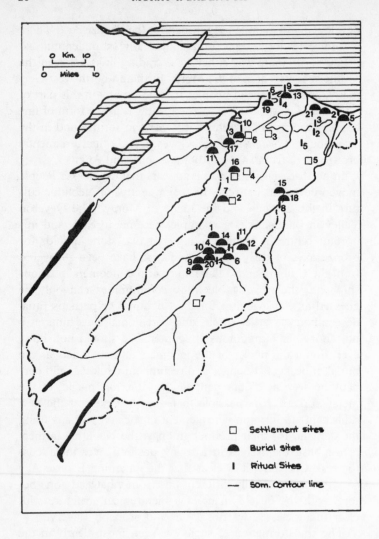

2. Bronze Age – settlement, burial and ritual sites

Kilmartin in Argyll, but no such examples have been found in Moray or Badenoch. Later, however, the cists were dug directly into the soil and, probably depending on the status of the individual buried there, a round cairn of stones was raised over the site. Without excavation it is impossible to prove, but the majority of round cairns from this region should probably be assigned to this era. Most occupy relatively prominent sites on skylines or hill-tops, as at *Tappoch of Roseisle* and *Inverugie*, the Roseisle example also seeming to be the most prominent element in what may have been a quite extensive cemetery. Others, such as that found in the 19th century to the west of Hopeman, stood in low-lying positions.

The stratification of the society which built these cairns can be seen in the character of the burials beneath them. The majority of cist burials so far found are males, and from the grave-goods buried with them they appear to be of high status. For example, the cist found in 1864 at Bishopmill in the northern suburbs of Elgin was 1.8m long, and contained the remains of an inhumation laid on, or covered by what appears to have been an ox skin, and a now broken grooved dagger. Amongst the most striking items to be buried in Bronze Age cists, however, are necklaces made of drilled and shaped jet. The finest of these from Moray came from a cist in what appears to have been an extensive cemetery at Burgie Lodge Farm (NJ 090606), now completely quarried away. A particularly fine grave assemblage from Culduthel near Inverness contained a beaker, flint arrowheads, a wrist-guard with gold studs, a flint knife and ring and 'toggle' of perforated bone. Later in the 2nd millennium BC, when Bronze Age society was itself undergoing a period of profound change in Britain, the fashion for burial was replaced largely by cremation. The cremated remains were gathered in pottery urns which were either buried directly in the ground or placed in small cists of their own, as at Bellie near Fochabers (see above p.14). The now destroyed burial mound at Kennieshillock (NJ 300 605) appears to have covered two cremations. The mound was raised over two pits 1.5m deep, which had been filled with stones. The bottom of one was filled to a depth of 5cm with a layer of what the excavator called "ashes", together with the sherds of a Food Vessel, covered by a flat slab. The second pit contained a cist with a Food Vessel and a flint, but while there was plenty of charcoal in the filling material, there was no trace of bone.

Until recently most of our knowledge of Bronze Age society has come from burials, in large part due to the 19th-century fashion for 'barrow-digging'. As a result, we have little understanding of their lifestyle as few settlement sites of early Bronze Age date have been identified in Scotland, let alone excavated. Finds of high-quality metal-work, such as the fine basket-shaped ear-rings of beaten gold found in the 19th century in a cist near Orbliston in Moray (NJ 301 585), or the 35 twisted gold ribbon armlets found in 1857 during ploughing on *Law Farm*, Wallfield point to a sophisticated and materially wealthy society, but no power-centre of this period has been examined in detail. In recent years, however, extensive projects in upland districts in advance of forestry planting – or after felling – have revealed large areas of former agricultural activity, now largely blanketed by peat. While some of these must belong to later periods, excavation of a few sites has shown that much of this buried agricultural landscape is Bronze Age. At *Tulloch Wood* near Forres, survey and excavation have uncovered the remains of an extensive area of plough cultivation in defined fields with attendant settlements surviving in the circles of stones which supported the timbers of conical-roofed houses. The nearby round cairn at *Califer* may mark the burial place of a local chieftain.

Most of the surviving areas of such settlement which can be traced above ground in Moray and Badenoch are at relatively high altitudes, e.g. *Chapel Hill*, Edinkillie, *Stony Hill*, Rothes, or *Whitewell*. Settlement at lower level has probably been a casualty of subsequent centuries of agriculture, but important areas have been identified along the southern slopes of the Lossiemouth-Burghead ridge, fringing the waters of Spynie Loch, and in the district around Fochabers, while extensive areas of field-clearance can still be seen on the valley-floor of the Spey to the west of the Neolithic cairn at Granish (see above p.12). Excavation of a midden in the Culbin Sands represents the only positively identified low-level Bronze Age domestic site, occupied temporarily on two occasions between 1400 and 1100 BC. Amongst the midden debris were the bones of cattle, sheep and pigs, cereal grains, and sea-shells, as well as sherds of coarse, undecorated pots. In the upland cases, the sites appear to have been abandoned in the late 2nd millennium BC, probably due to a marked deterioration in the climate after *c.*1200 BC which saw colder summers and a general increase in rainfall. As a result, there was probably competition for good land, with famine an ever-present threat. It is surely no coincidence that in the later Bronze Age weapons become increasingly common as grave-goods or buried in hoards of metal-work, and it is probably in this phase that competition over land in what may have been a struggle for survival saw the final creation of a stratified society dominated by a warrior-aristocracy. It is probably to the late Bronze Age, moreover, that we should date the first moves towards the large-scale development of major defended sites as individual tribes sought to protect their crops and stock.

Ritual monuments of undoubtedly Bronze Age date are equally rare in this region, but the cave site at *Covesea* forms a so far unique example of its type in Scotland. The stone circle building tradition had been in decline in the late Neolithic period, with circles becoming smaller and smaller in diameter and the number of component stones in the ring gradually reducing. While circle-building did not entirely disappear, by the 2nd millennium BC small 'circles' with diameters of little more then 2m had replaced the great rings of the Neolithic. The tiny 'four-poster' circle at *Templestones* near Forres is a classic example of the extremes which such reduction in scale could reach. It, however, is a unique example in Moray of a style found most commonly in Aberdeenshire and Strathtay, unless the heavily-damaged site at Browland near Garmouth (NJ 339 647) – not included in the Gazetteer below – represented another example of this type. More common in Moray and Badenoch are settings or alignments of two or more stones. At *Ballintomb* near Dulnain Bridge, an alignment of three stones runs along a gravel ridge overlooking the Spey, while at *Bogton* near Lhanbryde and

Pitchroy across the Spey from Ballindalloch there are fine examples of paired stone settings. The function of these types of monument are not certain, several theories – some quite far-fetched – having been advanced. Excavations at sites of this type elsewhere in Scotland, for example at Orwell in Kinross-shire, showed that they formed the focus for burial activity and for rituals. At Orwell, cists had been found during ploughing around the site, while the excavations produced evidence for several cremations. A role as places for local assemblies is another strong possibility. The Ballintomb setting formed the focus for the medieval law-court and rallies of the Grant lordship of Freuchie, perhaps representing the late survival of an ancient tradition.

Bronze Age Sites

Settlement

1. Chapel Hill, Edinkillie
NJ 03 47

Covering an area of some 10 acres of heathy moor on the eastern shoulder of the hill is a scattering of between 30 and 40 cairns. Two substantial cairns, 7.5m and 6.6m in diameter, appear to have been sepulchral, the larger surviving only as a robbed out ring of kerb stones. The remainder of the cairns are between *c*.3.8 and 5m in diameter and represent clearance of the ground for cultivation.

0.5 mile to the south (NJ 03 46) on the steep hillside above the wide, shallow valley immediately north of Dallasbroughty farm, is an extensive area of clearance cairns and hut circles which extends to the crest of the hill. Two circles lie close to the north side of the unclassified road and two further circles lie close to the summit of the hill, south-west of a conspicuous round cairn.

2. Dava Station
NJ 013 389

On the south-west facing slopes of the west top of Carn Ruigh Thuim, adjacent to the rough track from Dava to Aittendow farm. Heath fires here in the 1950s exposed large areas of the old ground surface beneath the peat and revealed substantial areas of cultivation interspersed with clearance and possible burial cairns. The areas of clearance, which can still be traced, are obvious as patches of stone-free ground bounded by 'rickles' and defined by the groups of rubble cairns.

3.   Pluscarden
NJ 142 580
A single hut-circle lies in forestry on the south-east flank of Heldon Hill, due north of the priory.

4.   Rochuln Rocks
NJ 068 462
A large field system with associated settlement lies on gentle west-facing slopes south of the Reenlarig Burn. Clearance cairns, 3–6m in diameter and averaging 1.2m high, lie to the north-east of a single hut circle, 9m in diameter, which occupies a plateau site.

5.   Stony Hill, Rothes
NJ 24 51
On the south-east flanks of Stony Hill, to the west of the A941 Rothes-Elgin road 2 miles north-west of Rothes. The easy slopes of the broad south-eastern ridge of the hill, between the two farm-tracks which climb the hillside from the A96, carry the remains of an extensive system of field banks and clearance cairns.

6.   Tulloch Wood, Forres
NJ 085 562
An extensive (27 hectare) area of settlement and field systems covers the upper slopes on the west and north-west slopes of Burgiehill. The footings of eight hut circles can be traced amidst a landscape peppered with field clearance cairns (over 250) and long axial banks which divide the hillside into roughly rectangular field blocks. These banks appear to be almost unique in Scotland on dated sites and bear close similarities to the axial divisions found on

Dartmoor in Devon. Here, as in the English examples, they seem to be the product of arable cultivation rather than being enclosures for stock. On the steeper ground to the south-west are a number of breaks in the slope which may be lynchets produced by plough cultivation.

Sample excavations in 1991 established that the earliest datable surface feature was an early Bronze Age clearance cairn. Much of the system of field banks is of later Bronze Age date, possibly associated with one of the hut circles which produced a roughly contemporary radiocarbon date. It would appear that cultivation was abandoned in the late 2nd millennium BC and that the settlement was re-established in the late 1st Century BC when further hut-circles were constructed. The site appears to have been abandoned finally in the 3rd Century AD.

7.   Whitewell
NH 914 087

At the head of the unclassified road to Blackpark, Tullochgrue and Whitewell, 2 miles south-east of Inverdruie. The eastern and south-eastern slopes of the rounded hill to the north-west of Whitewell farm have been intensively cultivated in the past, and more recent – and massive – field clearance can be seen in the fields immediately behind Upper Tullochgrue. The gentle slopes immediately east of the summit of the hill, which commands extensive views over Rothiemurchus Forest to the Cairngorms, are cloaked with heather and juniper scrub, amongst which can be traced at least four hut circles (the largest *c.*7m in diameter), plus several clearance cairns.

Burials

1.   Beinn Mhor, Dulnain Bridge
NH 998 277

On the south-west slopes of Beinn Mhor, 1 mile west of the head of the public road up Glen Beg and 0.75 mile west-south-west of Glenbeg farm. This heavily denuded round cairn stands at the south-east corner of a more recent farm enclosure (see below p.155) built from stones plundered from the earlier site. Positioned on the edge of a sharp break in slope, the cairn would originally have been a prominent skyline feature from the lower ground in the valley floor. The cairn is now little more than an amorphous heap of stones with no trace remaining of a kerb. In the centre, the remains of the cist are exposed.

2. Binn Hill, Lochhill
NJ 302 654

This overgrown round cairn stands in a forestry plantation on the gentle south-western slopes of Binn Hill, 2.5 miles west of Garmouth. It measures 10.5m in diameter and stands c.1.5m high within the remains of a boulder kerb. There is a depression in the summit of the mound which may mark the site of a 19th-century exploration of the cairn. There is a single stone 5m from the cairn, which may be part of a ritual arrangement.

3. Califer, Forres
NJ 079 568

On the west side of Califer Hill, 100m south-west of Califer Cottage. The plundered remains of a large round cairn, possibly associated with the settlement on nearby Tulloch Hill.

4. Clury, Dulnain Bridge
NH 972 242

Forming a pronounced pimple on the broad nose of the north-eastern ridge of the long range of hills which separates the valley of the River Dulnain from Strathspey, this cairn stands in the middle of a field formed in the angle between the unclassified road from Balnaan to Carrbridge, c.0.5 mile south-west of the bridge over the Dulnain. The cairn occupies an elevated position with clear views north and west over the Dulnain. Showing signs of considerable disturbance in the past, the cairn sits on a level platform which is probably a consequence of ploughing of the field in which it lies rather than indicating the presence of a berm.

5. Cowiemuir, Bogmoor
NJ 371 631

Three miles NNE of Fochabers on the B9104 and by-road to
Portgordon. Adjacent to the roadside fence-line, the denuded
remains of this cairn form a roughly circular platform, heavily
overgrown with whins, at the edge of arable cultivation. It has
stood on a slight knoll overlooking a narrow, shallow valley
cutting through the broad gravel terraces on the east side of
the Spey estuary. The superstructure of the cairn has been
almost entirely removed, probably for road metalling.

6. Curr Wood, Dulnain Bridge
NH 995 233

In forestry on the west side of the A95, 1.25 miles south of
Dulnain Bridge. The denuded remains of this overgrown
round cairn lie within the forestry plantation, 50m from the
road, slightly to the north-west of the hotel.

7. Dava Station, Dava
NJ 010 390

At the east edge of the forestry belt on the east side of the
A940 at Dava. A number of Bronze Age burials in this area
may be connected with traces of settlement and field systems
in the same vicinity. This cairn is straddled by the old parish
boundary between Edinkillie and Inverallan, forming the
boundary of the post-1974 Grampian and Highland regions,
and has obviously been used as a marker-post by past
generations. The cairn was excavated in the 19th century,
when it was found to contain two cists, a primary burial
centrally placed at ground level and a secondary insertion off-
centre at a higher level

8. Deishar, Boat of Garten
NH 928 201

Lying on a broad terrace in forestry, just below the 300m
contour on the south-east flank of the long ridge which
extends south-west from Creag an Fhithich, 0.25 mile north
of Deishar.

9. Drumuillie, Boat of Garten
NH 940 206

In forestry on the south flank of Creag an Fhithich, 0.5 miles north-west of Drumuillie.

10. Easter Gallovie, Carrbridge
NH 956 240

Lying on the terrace overlooking the River Dulnain, 100m north west of the farmsteading. This large cairn has been incorporated in the flood-dyke along the southern side of the river.

11. Hanover, (Kist Cairn), Newlands of Moyness
NH 971 531

In farmland west of Hanover Farm, c.2 miles south-south-west of Brodie on by-roads. This prominent skyline site has been a well-used feature of the local landscape for centuries, from the Middle Ages serving as a boundary marker on the dividing line between the sheriffdoms of Nairn and Moray.

12. Inchbroke, Grantown on Spey
NJ 045 257

In grazing land on the east side of the A939 Grantown-on-Spey to Tomintoul road, 0.3 mile south of the junction with the A95. This round cairn, 11.5m in diameter, lies just to the south of the crest of an elevated headland projecting from the south into Strathspey. It has been heavily robbed for stone in the past, probably for the building of the abandoned agricultural settlement whose foundations can be traced in the field between the cairn and the road. Despite that, however, its main features are quite clearly visible from the remains. A kerb of irregular waterworn boulders can be traced through the turf in various places around the circumference. The depression in the centre marks the position of a centrally-placed cist burial.

13. Inverugie, Duffus
NJ 154 687

A prominent feature on the western skyline from the B9012 Duffus to Hopeman road, this round cairn occupies the higher of two isolated, tree-crowned knolls at the east end of the Inverugie ridge. It survives as a flat-topped, grass-grown mound nearly 16m in diameter and 2m in height in an old shelter belt of trees on the east side of the farm track from Keam to Hopeman. In the centre of the level summit is a depression which marks the site of an excavation in 1859 which uncovered a centrally-placed cist. Small, irregular blocks of stone break through the turf in several places, but no structural features are visible.

14. Laggan Hill, Dulnain Bridge
NJ 008 268

On a sloping terrace below the upper slopes of Laggan Hill, on the west side of Glen Beg, 0.75 miles south-west of the head of the public road. Lying on the 380m contour, this superbly sited cairn commands broad views over Strathspey from the north. Like its neighbour on Beinn Mhor, it has been plundered for stone to construct the field enclosures which surround it, but it still preserves its shape clearly. Measuring roughly 13m in diameter, traces of kerb can be seen through the turf on the western side. In the centre is a well-preserved slab-built cist, measuring 1.8m by 1m, the two end slabs rising into 'gables' above the level of the lower side slabs.

15. Leakin, Knockando
NJ 164 420

In grazing land south of the track between Garlandmore and Leakin, running west from the B9102 c.0.5 mile south of Knockando. This round cairn has been considerably robbed for stone in the past. It survives as an irregular mound, 14m x 16m, standing c.1.1m high. Some kerb stones survive on the north and south sides. Near its centre a flat slab lies partly exposed, possibly formerly part of the cist, with around twenty cupmarks in the visible area.

16. Little Corshellach, Dallasbraughty
NJ 040 467

Standing on a south-facing slope, this possible kerb cairn has been extensively robbed for stone. It survives as a heather-covered mound 4m x 3m and 0.34m high.

17. Loch of Blairs, Altyre
NJ 019 554

In an area of former gravel extraction, amongst forestry immediately west of the A940 opposite the Loch of Blairs. Discovered during sand quarrying in 1931, this short cist, complete with its coverstone, was allowed to remain in place. In the cist were found the remains of a cremation and the sherds of a so-called Food-Vessel.

18. Mains of Kirdells (Bishop's Croft), Knockando
NJ 175 396

This round cairn occupies an elevated position on a prominent headland overlooking the Spey, west of the B9102 opposite Mains of Kirdells farm. It has been considerably robbed on its northern and eastern sides, but enough survives to show that it was some 10.5m in diameter and rises to $c.$1m high. Several stones of the kerb can be seen breaking through the turf on the west side.

19. Tappoch of Roseisle, College of Roseisle
NJ 145 673

This well-preserved round cairn forms a prominent feature on the summit of the Tappoch, the highest point on the long coastal ridge which runs westward from Lossiemouth to Burghead. In 1987 a substantial, well-built cist was revealed during ploughing 8m to its west. The massive capstone (1.88m x 1.10m x 0.17m) and the four lining slabs were all of local sandstone. The cist was aligned east-west and measured 1.10m x 0.70m x 0.55m internally, with a floor made up of carefully selected red, white and green quartzite pebbles. The cist contained the well-preserved skeletal remains of a tall male, aged over 45 at the time of death, lying on its right side, pointing west and facing south. The only grave goods were a burned flint core and a flint spall, and a patch of unidentified fibrous matter lay on his upper arm.

20. Toum, Boat of Garten
NH 960 217

Immediately to the east of the old steading at Toum farm, 0.5 mile north-west of the A95 up the farm track to Toum and Ouchnoire. This magnificent site is, without question, the finest of the remaining Bronze Age cairns in this middle portion of Strathspey. Standing on a sloping terrace which commands clear views to the east and south over the valley, the cairn structure still rises some 4m. The flattened summit of the cairn suggests that it may have been looted at some stage in the past, but the sides of the boulder heap show no signs of disturbance. There are traces of a possible kerb on the south side.

21. Wallfield, (The Law), Lochhill
NJ 295 653

This prominent round, gorse-covered bowl barrow (where the mound is composed of earth rather than stones, as in a cairn), an uncommon type of monument in this part of the world, forms a bold eminence on the summit of an isolated gravel hillock, 100m north-west of Wallfield farm, 0.5 mile east of Lochhill. It is 14m in diameter and stands 2m high, with the remains of what was formerly an enclosing platform 3.5m wide by 1.5m high surviving on the north side only. Excavations here in 1855 uncovered a central stone cist. This contained an inhumation burial with a Beaker, which is now in Elgin Museum, and five curved pieces of worked bone which had been pierced at one end for stringing. The cist was enclosed by an outer wall of boulders 0.9–1.2m thick, beyond which was a second circle of smaller stones. In 1857, about 100m west of the barrow, was found a substantial hoard of Bronze Age gold-work.

Ritual

1. Ballintomb, Dulnain Bridge
NJ 011 245

This alignment of three standing stones runs NE to SW along the crest of a gravel ridge between the line of the former Aviemore to Grantown railway and the River Spey, 1 mile east of Dulnain Bridge. The stones, which are irregular pillars, are positioned approximately 100m apart. In the later Middle Ages, this site formed the assembly place of the local courts, and the rallying-place of the Grants of Freuchie.

2. Blackhills House, Lhanbryde (Clackmarras Stone)
NJ 270 586

Standing beneath its own shelter in the grounds of Blackhills House, 1.5 miles south of Lhanbryde. The stone, an irregular pillar with two flat faces, originally stood at Clackmarras (NJ 270 586), c.1.25 miles west of Blackhills. As it stands it is 1.5m high, but it is reported to have been cut down in size. One face is covered with cupmarks. A crescent and a double spiral carved on the other faces of the stone are not believed to be ancient.

3. Bogton, Lhanbryde
NJ 274 607

This fine pair of standing stones, aligned north-south, are located on a level terrace, overlooked by higher ground to the east, in a field immediately to the west of the track to Bogton farm from the A96 at the east end of Lhanbryde.

4. Camus's Stone, Inverugie
NJ 153 685

Possibly repositioned as a central feature to be viewed from the south-facing windows of Inverugie House, this splendid monolith 1.75m in height stands midway across the straight edge of the semi-circular field which was once the south lawn of the house. It is incised with a single cup-and-ring mark. The grounds are private, but the stone can be clearly viewed from the roadside.

5. Coleburn, Fogwatt
NJ 243 547

Standing near the fence line in grazing land at the south end of forestry on the east side of the A941, 0.25 mile south of the turning for Coleburn distillery. This single standing-stone has been heavily weathered and may have broken. It now stands 1.4m high and is 0.6m wide at the base.

6. Inverugie
NJ 145 681

In farm land in the centre of the broad, dry valley between
the Tappoch of Roseisle and the Inverugie ridge are a series
of small rocky outcrops, about seven in number. Two of
these have cup-marks on their horizontal faces. The smaller
area is made up of about seven cups, but the second stone,
which measures c.4.0m by c.2.3m, is pockmarked with thirty-
three depressions, some of which have very worn rings
encircling them.

7. Lackgie, Boat of Garten
NH 968 210

Approximately 0.2 mile from the Neolithic chambered cairn
at Lackgie (see above p.13) The standing stones on the flood
plain of the Spey may be associated with the concentration of
Bronze Age burials along the southern flank of Creag an
Fhithich.

8. Pitchroy, Knockando
NJ 177 382

In farmland to the west of the B9102 Knockando to
Grantown-on-Spey road, 0.3 miles south of the junction with
the B9138. Shown on the OS 1:50000 series map as a single
standing stone, this paired north-west to south-east alignment
is placed on a wide terrace of level ground overlooking the
Spey, close to the fence above the steep roadside bank. The
south-east stone, an irregular pillar swelling out from a
narrow base then tapering to a rough point, is still upright
and forms a conspicuous landmark from the road. The
north-west stone has fallen over at an acute angle, probably
due to plough disturbance around its base in the past, and
now lies almost flat to the ground.

9. Sculptor's Cave, Covesea
NJ 175 707

At the foot of steep cliffs immediately to the west of the old
coastguard tower 0.5 miles north-north-west of Easter
Covesea. ACCESS TO THIS SITE IS EXTREMELY DIFFICULT AND

DANGEROUS, SUBJECT ALSO TO TIDAL CONDITIONS, AND SHOULD ONLY BE UNDERTAKEN WITH EXTREME CAUTION.

The sandstone cliffs running west from Covesea to Hopeman are honeycombed with caves which have served as dwellings and stores from at least the Bronze Age to the 19th century when they were last occupied by tinker families. The most important is Sculptor's Cave, so named from the mass of carving (and modern scribings) which cover its walls. The Pictish sculptures there are described below.

Excavation of part of the cave interior in the late 1920s produced a massive quantity of human bone, now lost, including the crania and cervical vertebrae, apparently severed by a sharp instrument, of several children. Along with these were found items of high quality decorative metalwork of Bronze Age and later date. These appear to have been thrown into a pool of standing water which occupied the rear of the cave, paralleling the ritual deposits of metal-work and sacrificial victims known from elsewhere in Britain and Europe. The discovery of the lower jaws from child skulls, grouped near the cave entrance, plus stakeholes for what may have been wooden-framed racking, has led to the suggestion that the heads were displayed on stakes until the flesh had rotted and the jaws fallen off, whereupon the crania would be placed for display on the racks. The cave certainly seems to have had some long-lived ritual significance which lasted into the Pictish period and it is perhaps no coincidence that one of the principal early Christian sites in Moray should be located at Kinneddar, just over 2.5 miles to the south-east.

10. Templestones, Forres
NJ 068 569

On grazing land behind private housing off the unclassified Rafford-Burgie road. This tiny four-poster stone setting is a unique example in this area of a ritual monument found most commonly in Aberdeenshire and Strathtay, believed to represent the Bronze Age tail end of a tradition of stone circle building which began in the Neolithic. It consists of four stones, the tallest 1.4m in height, spaced at $c.$2m intervals. On the south-east and south-west sides can be seen clearly the kerb of a cairn which has been built within the area defined by the 'posts', but the upper part of the infill appears to comprise modern field clearance. The stones occupy a narrow shelving terrace on the western slopes of Califer Hill, and enjoy clear views to the north and west.

11. Upper Port, Grantown
NJ 054 292

In the field formed in the angle to the south of the junction of the B9102 Grantown-on-Spey to Knockando road and the unclassified road from Cromdale. This interesting group of stones stands at the edge of an undulating gravel terrace, bounded to the south and west by the valley of a stream. It consists of an alignment of two standing stones, positioned NW to SE, spaced approximately 20m apart. Approximately 100m to the SE, immediately adjacent to the farm of Upper Port, is a second pair of stones standing close together.

THE IRON AGE

*c.*700 BC to *c.*500 AD

At the beginning of the 1st millennium BC the technology of smelting and working in iron reached western Europe. From about 700 BC new settlers, the Celts, were introducing iron-making technology to Britain along with new styles in art, new techniques in bronze work, and new forms of fortification and settlement. As with the earlier Bronze Age migrations, there is considerable debate about the numbers of Celtic colonists involved, and whether the migration amounted to an invasion. While there is clear evidence for large-scale population movement in the 1st century BC from the Continent into south-east England, which itself caused displacement of the settled population within Britain, the first phase of Celtic migration may have been relatively small-scale and involved only the movement of small numbers of people. Nevertheless, the settlers formed a significant element in the population, and before the first Roman expedition to Britain in the middle of the 1st century BC their language had taken over as the common tongue.

Because of contacts – and conflict – between the Celts and the Classical world of the Greeks and Romans, we know more about the type of society in which they lived than we do for any earlier period. Roman writers describe the Celts as a tribal people with a highly structured society divided into a hierarchy of classes headed by warrior-aristocrat and priestly elites, but founded on castes of peasant farmers and slaves. Warfare played an important part in the life of the Celts, both between different tribes and between families within the tribe: raiding and skirmishing appear to have been commonplace. These are the drunken, boastful warriors whose deeds are preserved in the epic Irish poems, such as the great saga of Cuchulainn, their lives a ritualistic round of carousing, feasting and fighting. They were also, however, patrons of the arts, loving outward show and flaunting their wealth in personal adornment and lavishing it on the weapons which they bore. One very distinctive form of personal adornment from

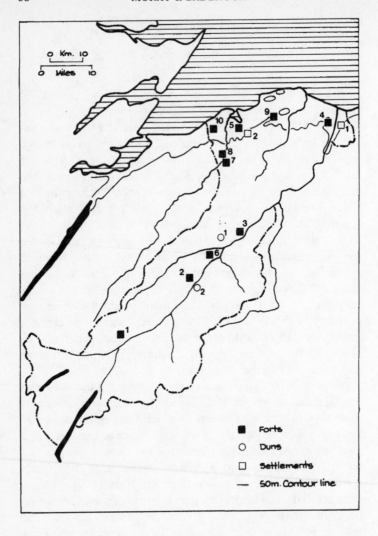

3. Iron Age – forts, duns and settlements

the north-east are spiral armlets of beaten bronze, the termi-
nals shaped like the heads of snakes. An excellent example
from the Culbin Sands near Forres is now in the National
Museum in Edinburgh.

Much of our evidence for the tribal structure of Celtic
Scotland comes from two important Roman sources, the *Life
of Agricola*, which records the northern campaigns of the Roman governor of Britain in the late 1st century AD, written by
his son-in-law, the historian Cornelius Tacitus, and the famous map produced at Alexandria by the geographer
Claudius Ptolomaeus (Ptolemy) in the second quarter of the
2nd century AD. The evidence from both, however, is not so
straightforward as often claimed, and the map especially has
been the source of fierce debate. What can be said is that
Tacitus and Ptolemy produced an image of a country divided
into the territories of a series of important tribes, one of
whom, the *Caledones*, offered some kind of leadership against
the Romans. The divided society of the Celts was easy prey
for the superior Roman military machine, and even when
they came together in alliance to oppose the invaders proved
incapable of offering serious resistance (see below p.49). By
the late 2nd and early 3rd century AD, however, Roman
sources hint at the formation of the development of larger
confederacies of tribes amongst the Celtic peoples of northern Britain, the presence of the Roman threat stimulating the
formation of more permanent alliances. By the middle of the
4th century, references are made to a people called the
Dicalydones, a powerful grouping whose name implies some
kind of relationship to the Caledonians of an early period.
Out of this tribal confederation, it has been suggested, developed the people whom we know today as the Picts.

In north-east Scotland, Celtic migration may have taken
place along the trade routes from northern Germany which
had developed in the early part of the 1st millennium BC. It
seems to have been along these routes that the style of fortification most closely associated with the Celtic tribes of northern Scotland, the timber laced forts, were introduced from
the Continent. Such forts are distinguished by massive stone
defences which were reinforced by timbers which ran hori-

zontally through the ramparts. At some such forts the timbers caught fire, either accidentally or through enemy action, and their burning generated sufficient heat in the heart of the rampart to cause the stone to melt and fuse. Sites which have undergone this process are known as vitrified forts. The only clearly early timber-laced fort in Moray and Strathspey is the first phase at the *Doune of Relugas*, but it is possible that a number of less well-preserved or unexcavated sites in the region may contain, or have once contained, an element of timber-lacing. It has been noted that in some fortifications the timber-work was restricted to the upper portion of the walls, which have now collapsed into shapeless heaps. Timber-lacing, moreover, was a long-lived tradition and at Burghead (see below p.58) timber reinforcing was used in the construction of the inner defences in the 4th century AD and later.

The development of fortification around major settlement sites was probably a response to the unsettled condition of society which had resulted from the sharp deterioration of the climate after 1200 BC. There is some suggestion that they may have served only as temporary settlements to which the local population may have fled in time of war and raids, abandoned in more settled times in favour of undefended farm settlements in the land round about, but several of the excavated hillforts, such as Eildon Hill North in Roxburghshire, were clearly occupied all year round. The state of our knowledge at present, however, does not allow us to identify the relationship between the forts and the outlying settlements, but they should probably be regarded as the centres of tribal power and prestige, the focal points for the people settled in a wide district round about. At some of the more substantial forts, which probably represented the centres of power of tribal rulers, the defences were probably in part intended for show as much as defence, being a display of the superior status of the builders. The elaborate gate structure from Cullykhan in Banffshire, or the carved frieze which may have crowned the wall of the inner enclosure at Burghead, point towards ceremonial display rather than strict practicality. At Burghead, the elaborate defences and scale of the fort may also be a reflection of a move in the later Iron Age towards larger tribal groupings, or confederacies, which formed the basis of the early medieval kingdom of the Picts.

Several of the forts are on a clearly smaller scale. Such sites, like *Allt a'Chaorainn*, may simply be a reflection of the smaller population of the highland areas, or, in the lowlands, mark a subordinate stage in a hierarchy of sites. The very slight defences to be seen at some examples, such as those at *Ballinlagg* where the fort's strength depends largely on natural features, or *Castle Hill*, Mosstodloch, would have afforded minimal protection against attack and were perhaps merely enclosures around glorified farm complexes intended as much to stop stock straying as to protect their inhabitants against raiding parties. Only two sites which display features characteristic of the stone-walled duns of the western Highlands and Islands, at *Beinn Mhor* and *Creag Phitiulais*, both in central Strathspey, have been identified in Moray and Badenoch. Such duns represent heavily fortified farmsteads consisting of a massive stone enclosure with timber buildings ranged against the inner face, perhaps occupied by only an extended family, and were built mainly in the period extending from the mid 1st millennium BC to the mid 1st millennium AD, and later. Their general absence as a class of monument from most of the north-east suggests that the two Speyside examples may represent a movement of colonists from the western Highlands into that region, possibly as part of the early migration of Gaelic-speaking Scots into Pictish territory.

Few settlements of clearly 'Iron Age' date, other than the major fortifications which served as the chief centres of population, have been identified in Moray and Badenoch. This is largely a result of the limited amount of field work undertaken in these regions, and of the difficulties in assigning a date to a site without excavation. Air photography in the west of Moray and in Nairnshire in the 1980s revealed large numbers of small enclosed settlements and concentrations of unenclosed hut circles – there is an important group on the flood-plain of the River Findhorn immediately to the south-west of Forres – but without excavation no firm date can be assigned to these. Excavation at the extensive field-system and settlement site of *Tulloch Wood* has shown that there was a partial reoccupation in the late 1st century BC after nearly 1,000 years of abandonment, and it is possible that other areas of Bronze Age cultivation in the upland zones may have seen redevelopment in the Iron Age. In general, however, there is a dearth of clearly identifiable Iron Age farming settlements, but the excavated crop-mark site at *Romancamp Gate*, Fochabers has pointed to the existence of a previously unrecognised class of unfortified house sites. The lack of defences at such sites requires some reconsideration of the traditional views on the turbulence of Celtic society, despite the fact that two of the houses were burned down in quick succession!

No sites of clearly ritual significance of Iron Age date have been recognised in Moray or Badenoch, although the important late Bronze Age 'shrine' at Sculptor's Cave, Covesea (see above, p.34) continued in use into the early centuries AD. There are few indications in Scotland, however, of 'temples' such as those identified in south-eastern England, apart from a little wickerwork hut which contained a crudely-carved wooden figurine of a naked woman excavated in the 1960s near Ballachulish in Argyllshire, and the focus of ritual activity seems to have been more on open air sites and natural features. Recent excavations at Deskford in Banffshire, around the site where the famous 'carnyx' – a bronze trumpet-mouth fashioned in the shape of boar's head, dating from the late 2nd century AD – was discovered in the 19th century, have shown that this was an area of marsh and pools of standing water into which the carnyx and other objects appear to have been thrown. The dumping of fine metalwork – cauldrons, weapons and jewellery – or ritual objects and sacrificial victims into boggy ground and lochs appears to have formed an important element in Celtic religious practice. It is possible that the elaborate rock-cut well at Burghead (see below p.60) may represent a continuation of this tradition into the later 1st millennium AD.

Few burial sites of Iron Age date have been located. From graves identified in various parts of the country it is clear that there was no single most favoured mode of burial. At Bellie (see above p.14) a series of inhumations, dated to the Iron

Age only on account of their relative position, were cut into the top of the mound which had been raised over the earlier Neolithic and Bronze Age interments. The so-called Pictish cemetery sites, identified by air photography at sites such as Alves and Greshop, were rectangular or circular enclosures surround low cairns containing a central cist-burial, may represent a long-lived Iron Age tradition.

Iron Age Sites

Forts

1. Allt a'Chaorainn, Newtonmore
NH 691 005

This small fortification encircles the summit of a prominent round-headed knoll on the west of the deep ravine of the Allt a'Chaorainn at the point where it breaks through into the lower ground of Glen Banchor. It consists of a single ditch and bank, eroded to the east where the slope has slipped into the gorge. There is no trace of internal structures.

2. Avielochan, Aviemore
NH 905 171

The remains of this fort occupy a strong defensive site on a rocky promontory overlooking the A9. Heavily overgrown with juniper and birch-scrub, it is still possible to trace clearly three substantial lines of defence. The outermost (western) line straddles the neck of the promontory and consists of a tumbled stone wall constructed of massive boulders. Beyond this, *c.*7m below the summit, is a second wall, now reduced mainly to a terrace. The summit is enclosed by a third ruinous wall which forms an enclosure 73m x 27m. The interior is cloaked under a thick covering of vegetation and no structures are visible.

3. Ballinlagg
NJ 079 328

This small fort occupies an elevated site overlooking the broad valley of the Allt Breac, about four miles north-east of Grantown-on-Spey. Positioned on the highest point of a hummocky promontory on the south-west slopes of Tom Mor, it is a site of great natural strength which has required limited defensive improvement. The elongated oval summit, a truncated cone in profile, is separated from the main promontory to the west by a natural dip. Across this, at the foot of the steep slope to the summit, has been thrown a rampart, surviving now as a broad terrace. This continues for a short distance round the north and south sides of the mound. There are faint traces of a second line of defence around the lip of the summit. The entrance breaches the outer rampart near its southern end and a distinct terraced track can be seen running from there to the centre of the west end of the summit.

4.   Castle Hill, Mosstodloch
   NJ 314 603

This structure, of uncertain date, survives as an embanked enclosure within forestry just north of the A96 road. The interior is approximately 40m in diameter within a low bank, enclosed by a shallow, 1m-wide ditch.

5.   Cluny Hill, Forres (Lost)
   NJ 045 590

On the south side of Grant Park at the east end of the town. Landscaping of the hill in conjunction with the building in 1806 of the Nelson Tower on the summit removed all but the faintest traces of this substantial fortification.

6.   Creag Garten
   NH 951 219

In dense forestry on the south side of the east ridge of Creag Garten, 1 mile north-west of Lackgie. There is no clear track to this site and good navigation is required to locate it within the pine-wood.

Provided with most of its defence by the crags of the flat-topped conical outcrop which it occupies, this small site formerly commanded extensive views south and east over Strathspey. The summit, which measures roughly 22m in diameter, shows no traces of buildings, and most of the rampart appears to have tumbled to the foot of the crags on the west, north and east sides.

7. Doune of Relugas
NJ 003 495

Strongly-positioned on a steep sided promontory just south of the confluence of the Rivers Divie and Findhorn, this small fort shows signs of occupation over a long period from the 1st millennium BC into the late 1st millennium AD. At the core of the fort lie the remains of a timber-laced rampart, enclosing an area 53m x 33m. This has largely been obliterated by the construction of a terrace and a dry-stane dyke associated with the modern house of Relugas, but several large masses of vitrified material remain, especially near the entrance on the eastern side. The natural strength of the site required no further elaboration on the east and south sides, but the easier approaches to the north and west have been defended by an outer rampart and ditch.

8. Edinkillie
NH 998 515

This heavily-eroded site, almost obliterated by ploughing, stands on the west side of the River Findhorn. Surface remains suggest a circular enclosure with a ditch and single rampart. The ditch survives on the east side of the site only.

9. Knock of Alves
NJ 163 629

The prominent conical mass of Knock of Alves, a detached western extension of the Spynie Ridge which divides the valley of the Lossie and its tributaries from the Laich of Moray, crowned by an early 19th-century mausoleum and monument known as the York Tower, forms a conspicuous landmark for travellers on the A96. While the summit itself is unplanted, the flanks of the hill on all sides are afforested, but several paths and tracks offer various lines of approach.

The fort consists of five lines of defence, probably not all contemporary and suggesting that occupation may have extended over a considerable period of time, possibly into the early Middle Ages. The innermost enclosure, 42m x 25m, occupies the summit of the hill, but has been largely obliterated by the 19th-century buildings. Only fragments of the enclosing rampart can be identified. This is enclosed by a second rampart 138m x 25m, outside which is a third line, possibly contemporary to it, almost entirely obliterated by the 19th-century access-road. Two further lines of defence, 6m apart, run round the lower slopes of the hill.

10. Muirside, (Downie Hillock), Brodie
NH 967 581

In a clearing amongst forestry, 250m west of the unclassified road running north-west from Brodie to the Culbin Forest. Labelled on the 1:50000 OS map as a 'Fort', this enigmatic oval earthwork occupies the highest point of a sinuous gravel ridge which runs roughly north-south through the woods. At its northern end the ground falls away steeply on all sides, but at the south gentler slopes connect it to the body of the ridge. The slopes show signs of scarping, but there is no trace of rampart defences, except to the south where a faint bank can be traced cutting across the neck of the ridge. There is no indication of the position of the gate, and the interior, which measures approximately 35m north-south by 18m east-west, shows no sign of structures.

There is no feature of this site which requires it to be solely Iron Age. Indeed, there is no reason why it cannot belong to a later period, and it is possible that it represents the seat of the lords of Brodie before the building of the stone castle on its new site 1 mile away in the later Middle Ages.

Duns

1. Beinn Mhor, Dulnain Bridge
NH 996 287

On a rocky spur on the eastern slopes of the north ridge of Beinn Mhor, 1.5 miles north-west of the head of the public road up Glen Beg. The tumbled walls of this dun encircle the highest point of a rocky outcrop, separated from the main mass of the hill by a broad depression. The wall has been between 2.5m and 3m thick, and sections of the outer face can be seen on the better-preserved northern and western sides. On the east, where precipitous crags offered natural defence, there are fragmentary traces of a less-substantial wall. The interior, which measures roughly 30m in diameter, is cloaked in heather and there are no traces of internal structures. On the north side, approximately 3m beyond the wall, a narrow and shallow ditch, running in an arc on the same curve as the wall, has been exposed in an area of heather-burning.

2. Craig Phitiulais, Coylumbridge
NH 930140

This site, identified as a dun, together with that on Beinn Mhor 12 miles to the north-north-east, lies far from any other monument of this category. It occupies a low, heather-clad mound, heavily burrowed by rabbits, in an elevated position on the west side of Strathspey, and enjoys clear views northwards down the valley. The dun survives as the spread ruin of a massive stone wall 10m x 6m and originally some 3.5m thick, broken by a single entrance to the south-west. There are no visible traces of mural gallery or internal structures.

Settlement

1. Romancamp Gate, Fochabers
NJ 356 617

In agricultural land west of the B9104 Fochabers-Spey Bay Road. This crop-mark site was fully excavated in 1990 and no remains are visible above ground. It has been included in this list due to its importance as the first of a new class of settlement site identified in this area.

The site was located through air photography and appeared as a three rings of what appeared to be pits, one much larger than the others, standing on the edge of a gravel terrace overlooking the Spey. Such pit circles had been identified in various parts of the country, with the greatest concentration west of the Spey and most especially in the district around Inverness, but there was no firm identification of age or function. It had been argued that they were Neolithic or Bronze

Age ritual or burial sites, or Iron Age houses, but most archaeologists were agreed that the pits were the settings which
had held upright timber posts.

Excavation of the largest of the circles showed it to be the
remains of a substantial round house – or rather there were
four successive houses almost directly superimposed one over
the other – dating from *c.*100–300 BC. The houses seem to
have been built in quick succession, the second and third
ones having been burned down. There were no defences
around the house, making this the first excavated, non-defen-
sive settlement site in this part of Scotland.

There was no clear evidence for the physical environment
in which the huts stood, but the line of a wooden fence, possibly part of an enclosure for stock, was traced. Barley grains
were recovered in the course of the excavation, indicating
that the gravel terrace around the site was probably used for
cereal cultivation.

2.   Tulloch Wood, Forres
   ### NJ 085 562

A single hut circle of Iron Age date was identified in the
course of excavations in the extensive Bronze Age field
system which lies south-east of Califer (see above p.25).

ROMAN

*c.*83 AD to *c.*86 AD

In the year 78 AD the Roman governor of Britannia, Gnaeus Julius Agricola, began a series of campaigns which were intended to complete the conquest of the British mainland. By 80, the Romans had reached the Tay in a reconnaissance campaign, backed the following year by the establishment of a chain of forts across the Forth-Clyde isthmus. There was brief respite for the lands beyond the Tay in 82, when Agricola attacked the tribes of south-west Scotland, but in preparation for a continuation of the northward drive the next year, a fleet was sent to explore the Hebrides. By the end of the campaign season in 83 the Roman army had possibly reached as far as Aberdeen, and the new conquests were secured by the construction of a strong line of forts running along the southern edge of the Highlands, centred on the legionary fortress of Inchtuthill on the Tay south of Dunkeld. From this advanced position, Agricola was poised to enter the last major area of good agricultural land and dense native population in the district along the south side of the Moray Firth.

In 84 the Romans began to push north-west from the coast near Aberdeen, intent on forcing a final confrontation with the tribal confederation of the Caledonians which had come together to resist them. Sending his fleet to ravage the fertile coastlands from which the Caledonians drew their supply, the raids carrying them first to Orkney and then ultimately to sail round to the west, Agricola aimed to force his opponents to chose between starvation and battle. At *Mons Graupius*, a site which has not yet been identified with certainty, but with Bennachie in Aberdeenshire and Knock Hill at the Pass of Grange in Banffshire being the most favoured locations, the Caledonians under their war-leader, Calgacus, opted to give battle and were crushingly defeated. There is considerable debate over the immediate aftermath of the battle, but the balance of evidence supports the view that Agricola pushed on to the west, intent on completing the task of conquest.

Although it is now argued as likely that Agricola returned to his bases in central Scotland via the valleys of the Spey and Tay rather than merely retracing his steps back through Strathmore, the traditional distribution maps showing Roman military sites in northern Scotland draw a final line at Bellie on the east bank of the Spey near Fochabers, a small site whose identification as Roman has been challenged, or further east at Auchinhove or Muiryfaulds near the Pass of Grange. Beyond that point, it was believed, the Romans did not undertake any significant land-based campaign. It is probable, however, that Agricola pressed home the advantage which his victory had brought, continuing his campaign along the Moray coast towards the head of the Firth and occupying this, the heartland of resistance in the north. Indeed, it is likely that he was preparing for a final drive into the northernmost districts of the mainland when word of his recall was brought from Rome.

Evidence for such a campaign is not generally accepted, but air photography and trial excavation have identified two sites west of the Spey in Moray at Thomshill near Elgin and at Balnageith outside Forres, with a third at Easter Galcantray near Nairn and a fourth at Tarradale on the north shore of the Beauly Firth in the Black Isle. These sites display clear Roman characteristics in the shape of the ditched enclosures, and excavations at Thomshill and Tarradale have unearthed what appear to be classic Roman military ditches. Unfortunately, however, all the sites have been subject to severe erosion through a combination of cultivation of the sandy soils on which they stood, wind action, and catastrophic flood, and internal structures have been reduced to the merest of vestigial traces as a result. In addition, the absence of any unmistakably Roman artifact material from the sites has made positive identification as Roman encampments or temporary fortifications as yet unverifiable.

All things being equal and these sites are accepted as Roman, their occupation must have been of very short duration, certainly no more than three years. By the time of Agricola's recall to Rome, pressure was already mounting on the Empire's Danube frontier and in 85 and 86 military crises there

forced the recall of troops from Britain. The withdrawal of
one legion and supporting auxiliary troops in late 86 left a
gaping hole in the military establishment in the island, and
the overstretched garrison which remained could not be expected to hold on to the advanced position achieved under
Agricola. As a result, the forts north of the Tay were abandoned and a temporary frontier fixed on the Forth-Clyde
isthmus, later pulled back to the Tyne-Solway line. When the
Romans returned to Scotland in the 140s, they pushed no
further than the Tay, and although subsequent campaigns in
the early 3rd century reached far into the north east, at no
time after 87 did the Romans aim for the permanent conquest and occupation of the north.

Camps

*The three possible Roman sites identified in Moray have left no
visible traces on the ground, being recognised from crop- and
parch-marks in air photography.*

1. **Bellie, Fochabers**
    NJ 355 651

2. **Balnageith, Forres**
    NJ 024 578

3. **Thomshill, Birnie**
    NJ 210 573

PICTISH AND EARLY MEDIEVAL PERIODS

*c.*500 to *c.*1100

By the beginning of the 6th century, the lands along the southern coast of the Moray Firth, especially in Moray itself and in the district around Inverness, had become the major centre of power in Scotland north of the Forth-Clyde line. This was the heartland of the northern Picts, the descendants of the Caledonian tribes which had fused into the northern of the two great confederacies which had opposed Septimius Severus in the early 3rd century. More remote from the risk of Roman raids into its territory, the northern confederacy managed to establish a political supremacy over the south, although the latter possessed greater wealth and a larger population. This domination was recognised by the incoming Scottish settlers of Argyll, for it was to the king of the northern Picts, Bridei, that St. Columba travelled in search of a diplomatic understanding which would ensure the survival of the fledgling kingdom of Dalriada. Sadly, only the barest skeleton of a history of this northern Pictish kingdom can be reconstructed from the fragmentary sources which remain, and there are few monuments which survive above ground to bear witness to the greatness of its culture.

Columba's mission to Bridei in 565 is the first historical episode in this region to which a certain date can be ascribed. Tradition ascribes to him the conversion of the king and his court to Christianity, but it is clear from later events that the northern Picts remained largely – and aggressively – pagan until the early 8th century. The great concentration in this region of Class I Pictish symbol stones, which carry no Christian images, is probably due to the lateness of widespread conversion amongst the northern Picts. The finest Class I stone from Moray, that from Easterton of Roseisle near Burghead, is now on display in the National Museum in Edinburgh, but other good examples can be seen in *Elgin Museum* and just outside the region under consideration in this book at Inveravon and Mortlach.

The scene of Bridei's encounter with Columba is usually

identified with either Urquhart Castle on Loch Ness, where a large fortified site of Pictish date underlies the later fortress, or with Craig Phadraig overlooking the Beauly Firth immediately west of Inverness. Both sites, however, are dwarfed in scale by *Burghead*, which was clearly the most significant centre of power in the region. The concentration of Pictish sculpture in the vicinity of this massive fortification, the quality and scale of its defences, the presence of possible pagan ritual sites such as the Burghead Well and *Sculptor's Cave* at Covesea, and the identification through air photography of cemeteries at Alves, Greshop and Pitcairlie, together with an important group of burials excavated at Roseisle, clearly mark it out as the most important Pictish site in this region, if not in the whole of northern Pictland. It may be no coincidence, therefore, that the greatest evidence for the process of conversion to Christianity is also found concentrated in the vicinity of Burghead.

The limited amount of archaeological work undertaken in this region is largely accountable for the near absence of other clearly identifiable Pictish secular sites. The spectacular hill-top site of *Dun da Lamh* near Laggan, controlling the route through via Glen Spean to Lochaber in much the same way as Dundurn controls upper Strathearn and the routes west into Argyll, is normally assigned to this period. Earlier fortified sites, such as the Doune of Relugas, Knock of Alves, Cluny Hill or Avielochan (see above), probably remained important centres of power from the late Iron Age into the early Medieval period, but this would have to be tested by excavation. No sites of lesser status of this date have been identified positively. Many are probably overlain by modern farms and settlements, but air photography again is producing monuments which may represent the homes of the less exalted members of Pictish society.

By the later 7th century, missions from the major Celtic monasteries in the west, particularly those founded by St. Columba on Iona and St. Moluag on Lismore, were beginning to penetrate the pagan lands of the north. Early centres of Christianity may be marked by sites containing the element *annait* (meaning a monastery) in their place-names,

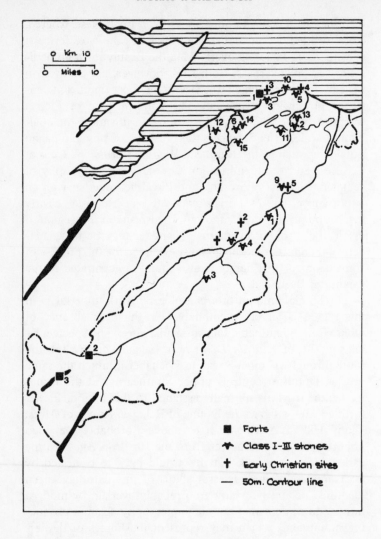

4. Pictish and Early Medieval – forts, Class I–III stones and
early Christian sites

such as the two *Auchnahannets* near Grantown, but no trace of early buildings survive at these sites. Their location in the central reaches of Strathspey suggests missionary activity from the south via Atholl and Lochaber. In the Laich of Moray, however, it appears that Christianity was spread from the important monastery at Rosemarkie in Easter Ross and it was probably from there that monks came to establish the monastery of *Kinneddar*. The abundance of sculpture from this site, especially of high-quality monumental sculpture closely akin to the magnificent examples from Nigg, Rosemarkie and Shandwick in Easter Ross, and its choice in the late 12th century as the (temporary) seat of the bishops of Moray, mark it out as being of major importance. Here, probably, was an important royal monastery and the centre of the local cult of St. Gerardine or Gerardius.

Birnie, to the south of Elgin, the first seat of the new bishopric of Moray established in 1107 (see below p.85), may stand on the site of another major early monastery whose cropmark remains have been traced to the south and east of the 12th-century church. Outwith these monastic centres, however, it is the Class II sculptured stones at *Brodie* and in *Elgin Cathedral* which mark the spread of Christianity, the Cross dominating the older Pictish symbols. Such stones, however, are rare in northern Pictland outwith the important monastic centres of Easter Ross in comparison to the south, especially Angus and Perthshire, a situation in large part due to the earlier conversion of the southern Picts. Their rarity, however, may also reflect a shift in the political balance within Pictland, with domination passing decisively from north to south in the late 7th century. Patronage of the arts which flowed from the court of a powerful and wealthy king may have withered away as the northern rulers were gradually overshadowed by their southern counterparts.

It is clear that a separate line of Pictish kings continued to rule over the lands north of the Mounth with greater or lesser degree of independence depending on the political situation in the south. When the southern kings were under pressure from their neighbours in Northumbria and Strathclyde, the northern kings may have enjoyed a renaissance of power. By the middle of the 9th century, however, a decisive change had occurred, the details of which we shall never be able to recover. At roughly the same time as Kenneth mac Alpin, king of the Scots of Dalriada, was establishing control over the kingship of the southern Picts, a second movement of Scots into Moray and the north was underway. This migration may have been spearheaded by Kenneth's rivals for power within Dalriada, the royal lineage known as the Cenel Loairn, for whom control of the fertile Moray plain may have been seen as a base from which to mount a challenge for the kingship of the Scots and Picts.

Despite the threat in the 9th and 10th centuries which Viking invaders posed to both Kenneth's descendants in the south and the Moray dynasty in the north, the two kingdoms rarely combined against their common enemy. Attempts by southern kings to conquer Moray usually ended in defeat and death: Donald mac Constantine in 900 at Forres, Malcolm I in 954 at the unidentified 'Ulnem', Dub in 966 again at Forres. It is probably as a monument to one of these episodes, or in commemoration of the earlier Cenel Loairn takeover of the northern Pictish kingship that the mis-named Sueno's Stone at *Forres* was erected. Gradually, however, the superior resources of the southern kings began to tell and a series of marriage alliances between the two dynasties served to draw the two halves of old Pictland closer together. A long-running and bloody feud within the Moray dynasty allowed the Scottish king to extend his authority further and at the time of his death in 1034 King Malcolm II could claim realistically to rule most of Scotland north of the Forth. Malcolm, however, failed to eliminate the Moray dynasty, a dangerous omission which was to have disastrous consequences for his grandson and successor, Duncan I.

The 10th-century marriage alliances between the two dynasties had probably been intended by the southern kings to eventually neutralise their northern rivals by absorbing them into the ranks of their own family. This, however, was a dangerous policy for a family which had a tradition of bitter feuds between its various segments, for the marriages created new lines of claimants who also cherished ancient claims to the kingship of the Scots. The rival branches of the Moray dynasty came together in the 1030s in the persons of Macbeth and his wife, Gruoch, both of whom could also trace descent from 10th-century Scottish kings. Faced with this threat, Duncan I marched north, but was defeated and killed in a battle located by tradition at Pitgaveny near Elgin. With no adult rival to oppose him, Macbeth was able to march south and take the throne of the Scottish kings in a dramatic reversal of positions.

Sueno's Stone apart, this dramatic ebb and flow of power in the period from c.850 to c.1050 has left no recognised visible trace on the ground. Despite the claims of local tradition and popular historical novelists, there is no reason to link Burghead with Viking activity – it is certainly not the *Torfness* of Orkneyinga Saga where Macbeth's fleet was defeated by Thorfinn, jarl of Orkney – and there is no evidence to support suggestions that Macbeth's stronghold was a crannog at Roseisle on the western fringes of the Loch of Spynie. Indeed, it is probable that Burghead was largely derelict in the 11th century and it is probably at Kinneddar, Birnie, or on Cluny Hill at Forres that we should be looking for evidence for 9th- to 11th-century activity.

In 1054, Macbeth's grip on southern Scotland was broken by Malcolm III, son of Duncan I, who with English support was able to drive his father's killer back into his ancestral lands in the north. For a further three years Macbeth continued to rule as king of Scots from his power-base in Moray, but, once he had consolidated his position in the Scottish heartland, Malcolm pursued his rival into the land that had been the graveyard of so many of his kinsmen. In 1057, at Lumphanan in Aberdeenshire, Malcolm brought Macbeth to battle and killed him, following this up in 1058 with victory at Essie in Strathbogie over Macbeth's stepson and successor, Lulach the Fatuous. Lulach's death is often portrayed as the end of the pretensions of the Moray dynasty to rule over all Scotland. In reality it marked the start of nearly two hundred years of bitter rivalry between his descendants and those of his slayer, Malcolm III.

Pictish and Early Medieval Sites

Forts

1. Burghead*
NJ 109 691

On the headland at the north-west end of the village. Despite the destruction of the greater part of the extensive defences which once cut off the headland now occupied by the village of Burghead, this remains one of the most impressive fortified sites in Scotland. Before the construction of the harbour and the laying out of the street grid of the present village in 1805–1809, three massive lines of timber-laced rampart, up to 6m high and 250m long, ran obliquely across

Figure 3. Burghead Fort

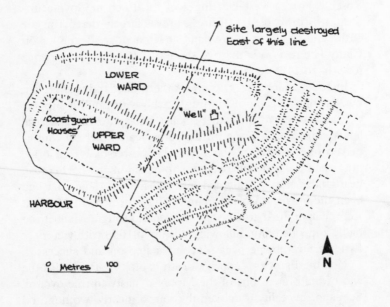

site largely destroyed
East of this line

LOWER WARD

"Well"

Coastguard Houses

UPPER WARD

HARBOUR

0 Metres 100

N

---- Modern Street lines
ιιιιι Slope of Rampart or ditch
─··─·· Northern limit of quarrying for harbour

the neck of the promontory from the south-west to north-east, the outermost fronted by a broad ditch. Within this, enclosing the highest area of the headland, was a yet more massive rampart, broken by a single entrance which lay approximately at the head of Grant Street. Its southern end was destroyed in quarrying to form the harbour, but its northern rampart and a short section of the eastern defences (forming a mound known as the Doorie) remain to give a striking impression of their former scale. To the north of this inner citadel, referred to as the upper ward, the ground falls away steeply to a level area of low lying ground, the lower ward, above the foreshore, bounded on its northern and western sides by the best-preserved of the sections of rampart. Excavations in 1890 showed the rampart to survive in places up to 7.5m thick and 5.3m high. The wall was faced externally by slabs to a thickness of 1m, but the inner face, c.1.1m in thickness, was penetrated at horizontal and vertical spacings of 1m by the ends of transverse beams up to 23cm square which ran into the core of the wall. These beams were additionally braced horizontally by planks of sawn oak, pinned to them by iron 'bolts'.

In the course of the 19th-century destruction, several pieces of sculpture were noted amongst the building debris. The most famous of these are the so-called Burghead Bulls, of which 6 survive from a possible total of 30 mentioned. These, as their name suggests, are incised sculptures in Pictish style of bulls (and cows). Their significance has been the subject of much debate, opinion ranging from the suggestion that they formed part of decorative frieze along the wall-head around the main gate of the fort, to their being ritual objects thrown into the coastal shallows from the fort to safe-guard the fertility of the herds on which its inhabitants depended. Two of the carvings are in Burghead Library, two more are in Elgin Museum and the remaining two are in Edinburgh and London. Also in Burghead Library are broken fragments of carving from an Early Christian corner-post shrine, similar in form to that found at Kinneddar and now in Elgin Museum. These were unearthed in the 19th-century in the small cemetery towards the top end of Grant Street, indicating that there was perhaps a Christian shrine of some importance in the area immediately outside the upper ward.

Perhaps the most striking structure to survive is the Burghead Well. This is a rock-cut chamber set at the foot of a low crag in the lower ward, originally lying to the north of a long spur rampart which ran eastwards from the north-east angle of the upper ward. It consists of a rectangular chamber *c.*5m square with rounded corners and 3.8m high, bordering a rock-cut pool 3.15m square and 1.25m deep, reached down a flight of irregular rock-cut steps. At the time of its discovery in 1809 its roof was broken and the present vault is a modern reconstruction. The steps have been re-cut and the pool itself deepened by explosives in 1809 (paving around the margins of the pool was also removed and the edge chiselled down in an effort to make it a suitable storage-tank for the village water-supply). Mistakenly described as a Roman well in the past, it has been suggested that it was an early Christian baptistery. The overall scale of the fort, however, makes it likely that it was simply a grand cistern in keeping with the rest of the site. An alternative suggestion is that it was some kind of pagan water shrine.

The complexity of the fort's defences suggest that it was probably not all of one period of construction and it would appear to have had a long occupation from the late 4th century AD through to the 10th century AD or later. Easily one of the largest forts of any period constructed in Scotland and far outstripping in scale and complexity the other Pictish promontory forts along the south side of the Moray Firth (such as Greencastle at Portknockie and Castle Point, Cullykhan, both in Banffshire), this was clearly a site of high status, possibly the principal political centre of northern Pictland.

2.   Dun da Lamh, Laggan
NN 582 929

Occupying a magnificent position on the easternmost promontory of the long ridge which divides Strathspey from Strathmashie, this superb fort has been interpreted as built to control the routes from Badenoch into Lochaber via Glen

Spean or the Corrieyairick Pass. Rocky slopes rise steeply from the afforested lower faces of the hill to the north and south in a single 200m rise to the summit, leaving the only easy approach along the spine of the ridge from the south-west, where a broad dip provides a natural defence before a final 25m rise to the isolated headland.

The single rampart follows the outline of the craggy out-crops which enclose the irregular summit area, 153m x 86m. The wall itself follows the contours of the slopes, varying in thickness from c.4m to c.8m. The entrance is believed to lie on the north, where there is an apparent break in the ram-part. In places the inner face of the wall, which is built of very small coursed dry-stone blocks, has been exposed to a height of 3m. Without consolidation or re-covering, it is to be feared that these areas will begin to deteriorate. Due to the irregular shape of the summit area, the wall has clearly-defined corners which have been constructed with great care. The summit consists of two rocky outcrops separated by a lower area of more level ground on which the settlement was most likely located.

3. King Fergus's Isle, Loch Laggan
NN 498 875

This tree-crowned rock, approximately 2.5 miles from the east end of the loch, is a prominent feature on the landscape to travellers on the A86 Laggan to Spean Bridge road. There is little visible under normal circumstances, the loch having been deepened artificially in the 1930s by the construction of the Laggan Dam, but in 1934 the waters were lowered by some 5m. At that time various finds were made in the loch-bed silts, including the remains of several dugout canoes. Investigation of the island, which by tradition was the summer hunting-seat of the early kings of Scots, demonstrated that it was not a crannog and showed it to have been occupied into the post-Medieval period, when the remains of a stone-built mortared structure had been fitted up as a shelter. This made use of the remains of an earlier structure, apparently a 15th- or 16th-century tower from which fragments of carved pine from a screen or item of furniture were recovered. This in turn overlay the remains of a much older building, built of clay-coated wattle, whose baked remains showed that the structure had been destroyed by fire. This phase has been dated tentatively to the early Middle Ages, but firm dating must await modern scientific examination.

Sculpture
(Class 1 Pictish)

1. **Advie**
    NJ 142 353

Set into the north wall of the vestry of Advie church, nine miles north of Grantown on the A95, is a weathered Class I stone. It is incised with a crescent and V-rod and tailed disc symbols.

2. **Birnie**
    NJ 206 586

In the kirkyard of the 12th-century parish church, near to the gate to the manse. A rough boulder, heavily weathered, incised with an eagle and 'notched rectangle and Z-rod' symbols.

3. **Burghead (see Fort)**

4. **Congash**
    NJ 058 262

On agricultural land at Congash farm, on the right hand side of the A95 two miles north of Grantown. This unusual site occupies an elevated position overlooking the River Spey. Described variously as a ruinous cairn or a chapel enclosure, Congash is a circular structure with a well-defined peripheral 'kerb'. The two symbol stones are positioned on either side of a break in the enclosure on its south side, and are well bedded in the turf making it difficult to see the symbols clearly. The stone on the left bears an arch and 'swimming elephant', that on the right a double disc and Z-rod and crescent and straight rod symbols.

5. Drainie
NJ 223 696

Twenty-six fragments of Pictish carving have been found in the old kirkyard, in the walls of the old manse, and around the important ecclesiastical site of Kinneddar. Most of these are now on display in Elgin Museum. The Class I stone has a crescent and V-rod symbol. The other fragments include sections of a corner post shrine of very high quality, its carving from the same school as produced the Hilton of Cadboll and Nigg stones in Easter Ross at the head of the Moray Firth. Such a shrine adds force to arguments that Kinneddar was an important monastic site in the late 8th and early 9th centuries, possibly the chief mission centre from which this part of north-eastern Scotland was converted to Christianity.

6. Forres
NJ 039 588

A fragment of a Class I symbol stone, incised with a portion of a crescent and v-rod, was discovered in 1992, built into the wall of a private house in the town. It is now in the Falconer Museum, Forres.

7. Inverallan
NJ 026 260

Built into the western wall of the old kirkyard, facing the Spey, is a badly weathered stone. It bears a crescent and V-rod and 'tuning-fork' and Z-rod symbol.

8. Kincardine Old Churchyard
NH 938 155 (defaced)

This stone, which bears a crescent and V-rod only, originally stood at Lynchurn (NH 951 206) two miles to the north on the opposite side of the Spey. It was brought to Kincardine in the 19th century for use as a gravestone.

9. Knockando
NJ 202 423

Set into the wall of the modern churchyard are two heavily-weathered slabs. The better preserved of the two bears incised crescent and V-rod and circular rosette symbols. A serpent symbol can be made out on the other stone, but any other carving is too worn for identification.

10. Sculptor's Cave, Covesea
NJ 175 707

The walls of the cave are heavily scarred by mainly modern graffiti, but amongst the carved nicknames and dates can be traced a number of Class I Pictish symbols which should probably be associated with the apparent ritual function of the cave in the Early Middle Ages (See above p.34). The best-preserved and most immediately recognisable are to be found on the walls and roof in the immediate vicinity of the eastern cave mouth. These include a mirror, a large crescent and v-rod, a 'lily' and a triple oval. In the east entrance there is also a large Russian cross, which may represent a Christian effort to sanctify a pagan site.

11. Upper Manbeen
NJ 185 576

On agricultural ground immediately west of the farm at Upper Manbeen, 4 miles south-west of Elgin by the B9010 and unclassified road. The stone has weathered badly, but is important in that it is one of the few where the symbols are set horizontally rather than vertically. It has a Pictish beast, a salmon and a mirror and comb.

(Class II Pictish)

12. Brodie (Rodney's Stone)
NH 989 584

Protected from the weather under a timber canopy, this fine Class II stone stands on the west side of the entrance drive to Brodie Castle. It was found in the early 19th century in the kirkyard at Dyke, indicating that the church site there may be of considerable antiquity. On the side away from the road it has a cross, while on the reverse are two 'lacustrine monsters', a Pictish beast, and a double disc and Z-rod, all carved in relief. There are three ogam inscriptions on the slab, now much worn, but that to the right of the cross transliterates as EDDARRNON, which may represent the personal name Ethernan.

13. Elgin
NJ 221 630

This stone, which now stands among the ruins of the cathedral, was found in 1825 when clearing the site of the old medieval church of St.Giles in the High Street, prior to the building of the present Greek-revival edifice. It is a rare example of a Pictish stone carved in relief on granite. On one face is a cross with the symbols of the evangelists in the angles between its arms, above a panel containing two fighting beasts. The reverse has rather cramped-looking double disc and Z-rod and crescent and V-rod symbols over a lively hunting scene of riders, hounds and deer. The top of the stone has been broken away, but above the symbols on the reverse survive a pair of hands grasping writhing tendrils, with a spiral-decorated disc between them. This has been interpreted as the remains of either a figure of Christ triumphant over evil (represented by the writhing serpents in his hands), or the pagan image of the Lord of Animals.

(Class III Picto-Scottish)

14. Sueno's Stone, Forres*
NJ 046 595

This magnificent sandstone slab, at over 6.5m high and weighing 7.6 tons one of the largest pieces of Dark Age sculpture in Britain, stands encased in its tower of glass and steel, signposted off the A96 at the east end of Forres. The stone has been the subject of various interpretations over the centuries, but there is now general agreement that it was erected between 850 and 950 in commemoration of the battle depicted on its western face. Just what that battle was, and between whom it was fought, however, remain the subject of much fruitless speculation.

It is the eastern side of the slab which is its chief glory. Here, set out in cartoon-strip form running from the top of the column down, are the opposing armies of cavalry and in-fantry, the conflict of champions, the flight of one side, and

Figure 4. Sueno's Stone, Forres
[Schematic drawing of East face]

the gruesome aftermath of the beheading of captives, piles of decapitated bodies with their hands tied behind their backs and stacks of severed heads.

The west face is dominated by a great ring-headed cross rising from a horizontal base. The cross and its background are filled with tight interlaced spiral knotwork. The lower third of the face is taken up by a badly weathered panel depicting what has been interpreted as a royal inauguration, with a seated figure between two tall, thin, bearded men, with smaller attendants in the background.

Unclassified Sculpture

15. Altyre
NJ 039 555

Within the Altyre estate 1.5 mile south of Forres on the unclassified Forres-Rafford road. This sandstone slab, bearing crosses in relief on both faces, was moved to Altyre from the Laich, possibly from near Duffus, in *c.*1820. It stands nearly 3.5m high, is 0.90m wide and 0.18m thick. The crosses have long shafts with the edge of the relief sculpture bevelled slightly. The heads are angular and stepped. The chief interest in the stone, however, is the Pictish ogam inscription cut into the lower left edge of the front face (with the better-preserved of the crosses). This reads AMMAQQAAH(or D) ALLMVBVMA(?)AHHRRSSUDDS, the first part apparently commemorating AM son of AHALL or ADALL. No satisfactory interpretation of the second half of the inscription has been offered. The sculpture is probably of the 8th or early 9th centuries.

Early Christian Sites

1. Achnahannet
NH 973 272

On the lower ground to the west of the steep slopes of Beinn Mhor, near the head of the unclassified road running north from the A938 1.5 miles west of Dulnain Bridge. All the structures to be seen in the vicinity of the present farm are of late 18th- or 19th-century date. The name alone survives to commemorate the early Celtic monastery (*annait*) which once stood here.

2. Auchnahannet
NJ 059 334

In the valley of the Allt Breac 3.5 miles north-east of Grantown. As with the previous site, there are no structures at the farm which occupies the presumed early monastic site datable to earlier than the 19th century.

3. Burghead, (see above p.58)

4. Kinneddar, (see below p.98)

5. Pulvrennan, Knockando
NJ 202 421

Adjacent to the old railway line carrying the Speyside Way 0.25 miles south-west of Knockando House. Early Christian incised stones were recovered from the site in the 19th century, but there are no obvious traces of structures to be seen on the ground. It is possible that the natural terrace in the sloping ground above the Spey has been artificially levelled to accommodate building. The name, Pulvrennan, has been identified as St. Brendan's Pool, suggesting a possible baptismal role for the pool in the river below the site during the early Christian mission work in this area in the 8th century.

THE MIDDLE AGES

*c.*1100 to *c.*1600
Historical Outline

The last four decades of the 11th century and first three of the 12th century were a time of major change in Scotland north and west of the Spey, but our knowledge of this period is limited to a few fragments which allow tantalisingly brief insights into the battle for control over this region. Indeed, it is difficult to construct a coherent outline of events, for these fragments produce conflicting pictures. What is clear is that the victories of Malcolm III (Canmore) over Macbeth in 1057, and his stepson, Lulach, in 1058 marked a turning-point in the history of Moray, with the initiative in the ancient struggle for domination of Scotland passing finally to the lowlands-based dynasty descended from Kenneth MacAlpin. Alliance with the Norse of Orkney and Caithness may have allowed Malcolm to extend his authority into Ross, but his grip on Moray was far from complete and Lulach's heirs remained in possession of much of their ancestral land. The Canmore dynasty's grasp on Moray slipped after Malcolm III's death in 1093, but was sufficiently strong in 1107 for his son, Alexander I, to begin the process of setting up a diocese for the province as a means of tightening royal control. The Scots may, however, have come to some accommodation with the native dynasty, for by 1130 power in the region was in the hands of an Earl Angus, a descendant of King Lulach.

Angus's ambition to regain the throne held by his ancestors brought destruction to his family and saw the beginning of the final Scottish conquest of the north. In 1130 he rebelled and led an army south in a bid to wrest the crown from David I, but was defeated and killed at Stracathro near Brechin. In the aftermath of this battle, David's army marched through Moray as far as Inverness and possibly into Ross. Unlike previous invaders, however, David intended his conquest to be permanent, and over the next twenty years established a chain of royal castles from Aberdeen to Inverness. The castles of *Elgin* and *Forres* formed part of this

chain. These strongholds were central to a more general colonisation which saw the development of burghs alongside the
castles before the end of the 12th century and the plantation
of settlers to create a new, loyal nobility. The most important
of these was Freskin, a Flemish knight to whom David gave
the lordship of *Duffus* in the Laich, where his great motte and
bailey castle, one of the largest of its type in Scotland, bears
stark witness to the military nature of the conquest and colonisation.

Despite a succession of rebellions down to 1231 led by the
MacWilliams, another family of pretenders to the Scottish
throne, the royal conquest of Moray was never overturned.
David's successors, his grandsons Malcolm IV and William
the Lion, continued the process and began to penetrate the
hinterland of Moray, pushing deep into Badenoch. It was in
their reigns that the royal burghs in the north saw rapid expansion, with Elgin becoming the seat of the crown's local
representative, the sheriff, whose courts became the main
source of justice for native and settlers alike. The towns, too,
were vital to the economy of the region, their privileged markets becoming the exclusive centres for trade.

The campaigns were mainly a co-operative venture between the crown and the Scottish nobility, military support
for the royal initiative being rewarded with land in the newly-
conquered territories. For example, by the late 1190s the
Renfrewshire family of de Polloc, vassals of the Stewarts, had
gained possession of *Rothes*, where the fragments of the medieval castle may represent the remains of their 13th-century
hall-house. Around the same date William granted Kinveachy
and Glencharnie on the northern fringe of Badenoch to Gilbert, earl of Strathearn, who in 1206 granted them in turn to
his son, Gilchrist, the probable builder of *Bigla Cumming's*
Castle at Boat of Garten.

The pattern of control was completed by King Alexander
II. He relied on the services of William Comyn, earl of
Buchan, to keep support for the MacWilliams in check, and
as a result the Comyns were to greatly extend their influence
into the central Highlands. In 1223 Alexander campaigned in
person in the north and a final burst of activity resulted. New

royal castles at Kildrummy in Strathdon and Urquhart on Loch Ness represented a tightening of control over lines of communication into and out of the Highlands, matched by the grant in *c*.1226 of the lordship of Abernethy, based on *Castle Roy*, to a son of the earl of Mar. It was the Comyns, however, who were the greatest beneficiaries. In 1229 Earl William suppressed a rebellion in Moray and following the defeat of the final MacWilliam rising and their total elimination in 1230, his family was given control of the lordship of Badenoch.

Of course, the Scottish takeover in Moray was not solely a matter of knights and castles. An important contribution was made by the Church, with the bishopric of Moray forming a key element in the structure of regional government. Although there was an ancient Christian tradition in the region by the 12th century, the establishment of the see in 1107 was the work of the Scottish crown, and the bishop of Moray was effectively a royal agent in a frontier zone. The first bishops had proven records of service in the royal household and were appointed by the king, who needed to be certain that the Church in Moray, which could have become a powerful voice for resistance to Scottish influence, remained firmly on his side. In conjunction with the new colonising lords and supported by royal legislation, the bishops were responsible for the construction of the diocese virtually from scratch. Their seat, fixed first at *Birnie* where the early cathedral continues in use as a parish church, then based subsequently at *Kinneddar* and *Spynie* before finally settling at *Elgin*, formed a base from which they oversaw the creation of the system of parishes on which local government was ultimately founded. Of these early churches only Birnie survives to give an indication of the appearance of a 12th-century parochial church, while the almost intact kirk at *Altyre* is the best-preserved 13th-century example.

The monasteries formed a second element in the ecclesiastical organisation of Moray. As with the bishopric, the abbeys and priories were part of the colonisation process and were linked closely to the crown. The earliest foundation, *Urquhart Priory*, was established *c*.1125–30 as a dependent cell colonised from Dunfermline Abbey in Fife, a monastery with close associations with the Canmore kings. The most important house, the Cistercian abbey of *Kinloss*, was founded in 1150 by David I and colonised from another monastery with strong royal connections, Melrose. Its importance as a colonising landlord was not solely political, for the exploitation of its vast estates as sheep-'ranches' and arable farms gave it a central role in the economic development of Moray. *Pluscarden Priory* was the last major monastic foundation in the region and symbolised the completion of the process of colonisation and the opening of a long period of economic boom. Founded in *c.*1231, it was possibly Alexander II's thanks-offering for final victory over his MacWilliam rivals.

By the 1230s, the northern lands had been drawn firmly into the sphere of the Scottish crown. The end of the long process of conquest saw the opening of an economic golden age, of which the still magnificent ruins of Elgin Cathedral are the most spectacular monument. Moray and Badenoch were integral parts of the kingdom, ruled by families who were amongst the greatest in the land, and tied into a trading network that channelled their produce into the markets of the North Sea lands. But in this prominent position lay the seeds of catastrophe, for when Scotland was plunged into the destruction and chaos of the Wars of Independence with England, Moray was to become a key battlefield in the struggle for mastery of the kingdom.

The defeat of the Scots and the abdication of King John in 1296 was followed by a triumphant royal progress by Edward I of England as far as Elgin, with sections of his army returning south through Badenoch and Strathavon. English garrisons were established in the key strongholds in the north, the old fortresses of the Scottish kings again becoming bases for a conquering power. Some local lords, such as Reginald Cheyne of Duffus, supported Edward, but others headed by Andrew Murray, a descendant of Freskin the Fleming, rose in rebellion and in the winter of 1296–7 drove out most of the garrisons. Their success was crowned in 1297 with victory at Stirling Bridge, but Murray died of wounds received in the battle. Defeat stung Edward into a massive response, and in

1298 he crushed the Scots, led by William Wallace, at Falkirk, but he was unable to rebuild the spectacular successes of 1296. The Scots, now led mainly by the Comyns of Badenoch and Buchan, gradually regained the initiative. In 1303 Edward mounted a major invasion directed chiefly against the centres of Comyn power, reaching Kinloss before turning south to take *Lochindorb Castle* and enter Badenoch to ravage the estates of the head of the Comyn family before moving down the Spey to serve similar treatment on the lands of the earl of Buchan. English garrisons were re-established and to ensure that the Scots did not simply recapture these castles in the winter once he had returned to England, Edward based himself at Dunfermline and prepared for a renewed offensive against the Comyns in the spring. Faced with the prospect of the devastation of their estates and seeing that Scottish resistance to Edward was on the point of collapse, the Comyns negotiated surrender on the best possible terms obtainable.

Edward's victory was overturned in 1306 when Robert Bruce, earl of Carrick, murdered John Comyn, lord of Badenoch, head of the Comyn kindred, and seized the Scottish throne. The result was civil war as the Comyn kindred, previously the staunchest defenders of Scottish independence, were forced to side with the English to avenge their murdered head. To secure his grasp on the throne, therefore, Bruce had to destroy the power of the Comyns and their allies. In the winter of 1307 he turned his attention to the heartlands of Comyn power and, marching up the Great Glen, launched a devastating campaign through Moray, attacking Elgin and burning the lands and castle of Reginald Cheyne of Duffus. In May 1308, having defeated the earl of Buchan and laid waste his earldom, Bruce had secured control of the north.

King Robert understood the vital importance of the north of Scotland for overall control of the kingdom: it had been Edward I's failure to keep the lands beyond the Mounth in his grasp which allowed the Scots to undermine his efforts at conquest. Such a strategic region had to be placed in trustworthy hands, and in 1312 Robert revived the title of earl of

Moray – in abeyance for nearly 200 years – placed under its jurisdiction the whole of Moray and Inverness-shire and awarded it to his nephew, Thomas Randolph. He was to fill the power-vacuum which the destruction of the Comyns had created, and provide firm government in a region which had lacked clear leadership since the 1290s. This new regime, however, had little opportunity to become established, for in the civil war of the 1330s between Robert's son, David II, and Edward Balliol, son of King John, the region again became a battleground in the struggle for mastery of the kingdom. Indeed, in 1336 Edward III of England pushed deep into the earldom, reaching Lochindorb Castle, and burned Forres, Kinloss Abbey and Elgin. The Randolphs, too, had little opportunity to consolidate their position, for they were involved deeply in the government of the kingdom during the minority and exile of King David, and the male line of the family was extinguished in 1346 when the third earl was killed in the Scottish defeat at Neville's Cross near Durham.

For the next twenty-five years there was no earl of Moray and by 1367 King David's nephew, the future Robert II, was in control of the lordship of Badenoch while Lochaber was coming under pressure from the MacDonalds of Islay. David had little interest in the northern parts of his realm and it was not until Robert's accession to the throne in 1371 that active steps were taken to provide a new settlement in the region. Robert's third son, Alexander, expected to inherit the earldom of Moray – he had been given Badenoch by his father in the late 1360s – but the title passed instead to John Dunbar, brother of the earl of March. John's earldom was a shadow of its former self for he was given only a rump of land along the Moray coast from the Spey to the lands west of Inverness. Lochindorb Castle and Badenoch were confirmed in the possession of Alexander Stewart, Urquhart on Loch Ness passed to his younger brother, David, and Lochaber slipped increasingly under MacDonald control.

The division of the earldom in 1371–2 proved ultimately to be a disaster. The Dunbar earldom, while rich, was dangerously exposed to raids out of its mountainous hinterland, the loss of Urquhart, Ruthven and Lochindorb stripping it of its southern buffer zone. Indeed, Earl John received none of the major castles of the old Randolph earldom and began the development of *Darnaway* as the new centre of his power. Alexander Stewart, lord of Badenoch (the Wolf of Badenoch), although built up by his father to be the royal lieutenant in the north of the kingdom, never enjoyed the undisputed power of the Randolphs and saw his position constantly undermined by the bishop of Moray, Alexander Bur, and by the jealousy of his brothers. Alexander's inept handling of power, and his disastrous personal life, involved him in long-running disputes with the kinsmen of his wife in Ross, with his own family over the lordship of Urquhart, and with Bishop Bur over rights of property and lordship in Badenoch and Rothiemurchus. It was the last which led ultimately to the burning of Elgin Cathedral by his men in June 1390.

The sack of Elgin was symptomatic of a general increase in lawlessness in the Highlands in the later 14th century, lawlessness which Alexander did little to curb and which his violent actions seemed rather to encourage. Throughout his career he seems to have exercised the wide powers with which he had been armed by his father only when it served his own interests, the most common complaint against him being that he did nothing rather than what he did being unlawful. In large part this was a personal failing, for he seems to have taken little interest in the exercise of good lordship over his once-extensive dominions, but it was a situation which the strong opposition he encountered amongst the old established families, and the interference of his brothers, served only to aggravate. If nothing else, however, Alexander had managed to hold together the central Highlands and prevent the more widespread destabilisation which the disintegration of the Randolph earldom had threatened. The slackening of his hold pointed to dark days ahead, especially when his local rivals, the Dunbars, failed to prevent the MacDonalds from filling the void which he left behind him, as was amply demonstrated in 1402 when Alisdair MacDonald, son of the lord of the Isles, led his men into the heart of Moray to loot the chanonry around Elgin Cathedral.

By the time of Alexander's death in 1405, however, steps were being taken to re-tighten the grip of the Stewart dynasty over the central Highlands. Soon after 1402 his eldest bastard son, also called Alexander, had married the widowed countess of Mar and by 1404 was using the title of earl of Mar and lord of the Garioch. A much more capable man than his father, and working closely in association with his uncle, Robert, duke of Albany, lieutenant of the kingdom for his brother King Robert III and regent for the captive King James I, Mar was built up as the new royal strong man in the north, a point underlined when he was placed in control of Badenoch and Urquhart Castle following his father's death. It was in recognition of this role as royal strong man that Donald MacDonald, lord of the Isles, attacked him in 1411 in his campaign to win recognition of his right to the earldom of Ross. Despite the severe mauling which his army received at Donald's hands in the battle of Harlaw, Mar remained the chief agent of the crown in the Highlands until his death in 1435.

Mar's death without heirs brought yet another change in lordship to the central Highlands and followed quick on the heels of the extinction of the male line of the Dunbar earls of Moray in 1429. To replace Mar, James I built up the power of the Gordons of Huntly. In 1436 they were created lords Gordon, and in 1445 his son, James II, elevated them to the earldom of Huntly with the clear intention that they fill the vacant role of royal strong men in the Highlands, an intention emphasised by the granting to them of the lordship of Badenoch. While their principal role was that of policeman in the increasingly ungovernable Highland zone where families such as the Mackintoshes were gradually entrenching their position, James II also used them to counterbalance the growing power of the Douglas family in the north.

The Douglases, the most powerful family in Scotland after the Stewarts, had begun to build up their power in a small way in northern Scotland in the early 14th century, but inheritance of the Murray estates in the 1360s had transformed them into powerful regional lords. Much of this inheritance passed to James the Gross, younger son of Archibald the

Aviemore, ring cairn.

Toum, round cairn.

Laggan Hill, round cairn and cist.

Beinn Mhor, dun.

Kinloss Abbey, entrance to refectory.

Brodie, the Rodney Stone.

Elgin Cathedral, east end.

Dallas, kirkyard cross.

Duffus, St. Peter's Kirk.

Lochindorb Castle.

Spynie Palace, Davy's Tower.

Duthil, kirk and Grant Mausoleum.

Edinkillie, railway viaduct.

Elgin, Braco's Banking House.

Quarrywood, doocot.

Garva bridge.

Hopeman, ice-house.

Grim, third earl of Douglas, and on his succession to the earldom in 1440 were used to provide for his younger sons. Having secured the marriage of his third son, Archibald, to the
Dunbar heiress, in 1445 Moray joined the earldoms held by
the Douglases and Lochindorb was restored to it as a wed-
ding present. Archibald's younger brothers, Hugh and John,
also became major landowners in the north, receiving the titles of earl of Ormond and lord Balvenie respectively. This
sudden spread of Douglas power was viewed with deep sus-
picion by James II, who was already on bad terms with the
earl of Douglas, hence his decision to build up the Gordons
to check their influence, but it was also deeply resented by
several of the more ancient families of the region who saw
them as unwelcome interlopers.

The tense relationship between the Douglases and the king
erupted in 1452 when James stabbed to death Earl William
during a meeting at Stirling. The murdered earl's brothers
rose immediately in revolt, Archibald earl of Moray marching
from Darnaway to destroy Huntly Castle, the headquarters of
the king's chief supporter in the north, burning Duffus along
the way. In response, Huntly, who had been marching south
to join the king, hurried back to the north and launched a re-
taliatory raid deep into Douglas territory in Moray. Although
peace was restored soon after, the relationship remained
tense and when James II finally forfeited the Douglases in
1455 and broke their power for ever, Huntly and other local
lords, such as the lord of Cawdor, took great satisfaction
from marching into Moray and seizing their property.

After 1455 the Gordons were confirmed as the dominant
family in the north-east, a position strengthened in 1475
when James III stripped the MacDonalds of the earldom of
Ross. Possession of Badenoch, where they rebuilt the castle at
Ruthven (see below, p.146), was augmented by control of the
lands of the earldom of Moray and much of Mar, and by
1500 the Gordons were clearly the most powerful family in
Scotland north of the Mounth, exercising lordship over many
of the emergent clans of the central Highlands. The Gordons'
grip on northern Scotland was unshakeable until the late
1550s, when, despite their Catholicism they had supported

the Protestant Lords of the Congregation against the Regent, Mary of Guise, and her French allies. As a result of this the Gordons were able to seize much of the property of the Catholic Church in their territories, but by the time of the Reformation in 1560 much had already been alienated by local churchmen to their kin. In this way, for example, the lands of Kinloss Abbey at *Burgie* passed into the hands of the Dunbar family.

On the return of Queen Mary from France in 1561, Huntly, the foremost Catholic nobleman in a kingdom which was already largely Protestant, perhaps expected to play a central role in any schemes which the Catholic queen might consider for the overturn of the Reformation in Scotland. It had been suggested to her that she should land at Aberdeen and, with the might of the Gordons at her back, impose Counter-Reformation on her kingdom. On the advice of her half-brother, Lord James Stewart, however, she rejected this idea. Further antagonism followed when Mary awarded the earldom of Moray, which Huntly was administering, to Lord James. Belief that he was indispensible to the crown as lieutenant in the north made Huntly over-confident of the strength of his position. Consistently outmanoeuvred by the wily new earl of Moray, Huntly rebelled, but was defeated and killed at Corrichie in Cromar in western Aberdeenshire. The fall of the Gordons was as dramatic as that of the Douglases a century earlier, their lands and titles being seized by the crown and their sumptuous palace at Huntly being looted. In their place Mary installed her half-brother, Moray, who was to become the new strong man in the north.

This new arrangement lasted only until 1565 when Moray fell from grace. To counterbalance his influence in the north, George Gordon, imprisoned since his capture at Corrichie in 1562, was restored to his father's lands and titles. Rather than balance, however, feud resulted, destroying the stability which Gordon dominance had provided, for neither Huntly nor Moray could assert local pre-eminence. The disturbed condition of the land, riven by religious and political dissension, can be seen, for example, in the new defences added to the old episcopal palace at *Spynie*, faith in God being replaced by certainty in the merits of gunpowder. The disturbed politics of the kingdom after 1567 ensured that the struggle continued into the 1590s under the heirs of the rival earls. Families such as the Grants of Freuchie and the Mackintoshes of Dunnachton, both powerful lineages in Badenoch, had long resented the power of the Gordons and by siding with the earl of Moray ensured the destabilisation of the region. Only when Huntly was able to attract them back to his side was the balance of power shifted again decisively in his favour, and even then it was only the brutal murder of Moray at Donibristle in Fife in February 1592 that brought the affair to a conclusion.

Medieval Sites

Cathedrals, Abbeys, Priories and Parish Churches

The Scottish cathedrals and abbeys are amongst the most impressive monuments built in the Middle Ages. Their scale speaks not only of the wealth which was lavished on them, but points also to the deep piety of the faithful who believed that their generosity to the Church secured them quick passage to Heaven. The expenditure on these great buildings, however, had another consequence in a relatively poor kingdom like Scotland: few parish churches outside the important burghs were ever built on a scale comparable to those of England. The result was that few of the rural parish churches of the Middle Ages ever developed much beyond their original simple layout, and while many of the surviving church buildings may appear now to be largely 18th- or 19th-century in date, in many cases they are either built on more ancient foundations, or the existing walls are largely of ancient fabric with only newer, larger windows and doorways – the datable features – inserted in place of the old forms.

The earliest church buildings to survive in Moray and Badenoch date from the 12th century. Some, like *Birnie*, may overlie more ancient structures, and at *Kinneddar*, for example, pre-12th century remains may be overlain by the site of the later castle and churchyard. The medieval buildings which remain were the product of the Roman Catholic man-

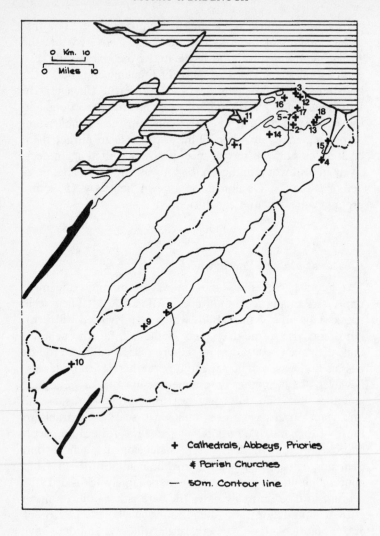

5. The Middle Ages – cathedrals, abbeys, priories and
parish churches

ner of worship which had finally established its primacy in Scotland in the late 11th century, replacing the older Celtic Church. In the course of the 11th and 12th centuries, the Roman Church was experiencing an internal reformation which saw a great upsurge in spiritual zeal and piety. This saw attempts to free the government of the Church from the influence of worldly rulers, and also generated a great outburst of reforming moves to purge the Church of corruption and abuses. From this developed all the great religious orders of monks and canons of the Middle Ages, each successive order claiming to be more pure and closer to God than the last. These new orders began to be introduced into Scotland in the late 11th and early 12th centuries when the reforming movement was at its height, and were to be used by the kings of Scots to provide the rigorous new bishops who reorganised their national Church and to spread the Continental-style organisation throughout the kingdom.

Amongst the most influential of these new orders were the Cistercians, named after the abbey of Citeaux in France. They were especially favoured by David I and his heirs. David founded the first Cistercian abbey in Scotland in 1136 at Melrose in Roxburghshire, and by the time of his death in 1153 Melrose had sent out colonies, under David's direction, to Newbattle in Midlothian, Holmcultram in Cumberland, and *Kinloss* in Moray. The Cistercians were a particularly austere order who sought escape from the lures of the world in remote places away from towns and villages, devoting themselves to God through hard labour on the land and a daily round of prayer and worship. At first, they could not accept gifts of property which tied them to worldly things – like control of a parish church, or of a mill, or of the right to rents from tenanted property – seeking instead land which they could farm and exploit purely for their own support. As a result, they became pioneering agriculturalists, and are traditionally seen as the colonists and frontiersmen of the Church. Gradually, however, the original spirituality of the Cistercians waned, and newer orders with a better reputation gained popularity in their stead. One such was the Valliscaulian, a minor order with only three monasteries in

Scotland, the most important of which was at *Pluscarden*.

In the course of the 13th century fewer and fewer monasteries were founded. This was in part due to the great cost involved in such a venture for the person founding the monastery, for few of even the most noble families possessed the resources necessary, but was also a consequence of popular awareness of the decline in the religious standards of the monks and canons. Instead, the new orders of friars began to grow in popularity, their simple lifestyle and personal poverty harking back to the purity and simplicity of the early monks. Perhaps more important, however, was the fact that it was cheaper to found a friary than a major monastery. *Elgin* had two friaries (Franciscan and Dominican) by the end of the Middle Ages, the church of the Franciscan friary surviving in use as the chapel of a convent of nuns. The only other friary established in this region was a house of Carmelites at *Kingussie*, founded in the late 15th century.

The greatest of all the religious buildings in Moray was the cathedral at *Elgin*. Earlier and smaller cathedrals – the church where the bishop of Moray had his base – had been at *Birnie*, *Kinneddar* and *Spynie*, but in the 1220s the decision was taken to site the bishop's church beside Elgin, which was already probably the more prosperous of the two burghs of Moray. The cathedral was not a monastery, but was served by a college of secular canons, that is priests who did not belong to one of the religious orders. They formed the chapter of the cathedral and diocese, essentially the management committee of important clergy responsible to the bishop for the routine administration of the bishopric. To support them, revenues were assigned from particular parishes. In theory, the cathedral dignitaries, or prebends, were priests of the parish from which they drew their income, but in reality few ever served the local parish church and appointed a vicar or curate to fulfil their duties.

The parishes were the basic unit on which the whole structure of the Church was built. The pattern of parishes in Moray diocese was largely created in the later 12th century, once the region had been brought under the political control of the Scottish crown. While some parishes, such as the group in central Strathspey centred on Kingussie and Inch, may have had their origin in ancient chapels associated with the cult of Celtic saints, such as Drostan at *Kincraig*, most appear to have their origins in the lordships created by the Scottish kings for incoming colonists, the boundaries of the secular and ecclesiastical units often being co-terminous. These lords were used to a system in England and on the Continent which saw the church buildings being paid for and built by the local lord, who would also assign land or revenues to it for the support of a priest. Having essentially paid for the church, the lord would control the right to appoint the priest, who would often be his chaplain and might even be a member of his own family. Such churches as *Duffus*, founded by the descendants of Freskin the Fleming, or *Altyre*, probably founded by the Comyns, are typical of this process. Over time, however, the lords were persuaded to grant away the right of patronage – as the appointment of the priest was called – often bestowing it as a gift on a monastery or cathedral in return for the promise of salvation in the hereafter and the saying of perpetual masses on behalf of his soul. Gradually, however, the right of patronage was extended into control of the revenues of the parish – a process known as appropriation – and money was diverted away from the parish churches for the support of the monasteries which controlled those rights. The result was a starvation of revenue at local level and many churches fell into disrepair for want of funds, this being one of the chief complaints of the Reformers at the time of the Reformation in the 16th century.

Another consequence of the appropriation of revenues from the parishes was that there was little money left to support the vicar or curate appointed to provide services. Ambitious clerics were unlikely to be interested in serving as parish priests, with the result that the parishes came to be served by men of poorer quality, often with a minimal education and only able to read the Latin services but not understand them. This decline in spiritual life at parish level was a recognised abuse and the bishops, who were ultimately responsible for the provision of services in their diocese, often made attempts to ensure that stipends were fixed at a level that would attract a better class of priest into the parishes. In some areas, the friars offered a preaching service which compensated to some extent for the poor standards amongst the clergy, but in general, outwith the major burghs the quality of priestly care was very poor by the later Middle Ages.

It is wrong, however, to paint an entirely black picture of the pre-Reformation Church. Abuses and corruption there certainly were, but even on the eve of the overthrow of the old hierarchy in 1560 some influential clergy were attempting reform from within. Men such as Bishop William Elphinstone of Aberdeen, or Thomas Chrystall and Robert Reid, abbots of Kinloss, sought to improve the standards of education amongst their priests and monks and to improve the standards of religious life generally. How successful such moves might have been we shall never know, for the first half of the 16th century saw a gathering momentum behind pressure for radical change. By the 1540s the Lutheran reform movement had many supporters in Scotland, and in 1560 the Protestants were able to seize the political initiative and forced an Act of Reformation through parliament. Despite this victory on paper there was no sudden transformation along the lines of the English Reformation, and in some areas, such as north-east Scotland, where the aristocracy remained largely Roman Catholic, little action was taken. Rather than a Dissolution of the Monasteries, as undertaken by Henry VIII, the abbeys and priories were left to wither away, their communities slowly dying and not being replaced. Few of the great churches were actively destroyed by the reformers, but were instead left to fall into decay through neglect and starvation of funds. Elgin Cathedral remained largely intact until the 17th century, but the lead had been stripped from its roof and once the timbers rotted and collapsed the ruin of the building proceeded rapidly.

1.　Altyre
NJ 036 554

The well-preserved roofless ruin of the 13th-century parish church, abandoned since the 1650s, stands amongst trees in the walled policies of the now demolished Altyre House. The church is a plain rectangle, originally with no external buttresses. The north and south walls are pierced near their west end by plain, pointed-arched doorways and there are two slender lancets in the north wall and three in the south. The eastern of the south windows is positioned to throw side illumination on the site of the altar. The east gable is pierced centrally by a single tall lancet with simple Y-tracery. There is no window in the west gable.

2. Birnie
NJ 206 587

2.5 miles south of Elgin on the unclassified road between New Elgin and the B9010 Elgin to Dallas road. In 1107 King Alexander I began moves for the establishment on a regular basis of a new bishopric for the region. The first bishops fixed their seat at Birnie, where there was probably a pre-existing church dedicated to St. Brendan. Birnie remained the cathedral of the diocese until 1184, when the bishop moved his seat to Kinneddar.

The structure of the church remains much as originally set out, with the nave having been reduced in length in 1734 by only a few feet and new, large windows inserted on its south side. The church, constructed throughout of fine ashlar

Figure 5. Birnie Kirk

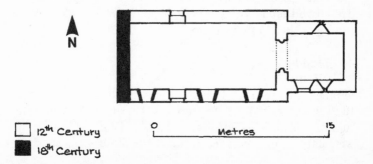

N

☐ 12ᵗʰ Century
■ 18ᵗʰ Century

0   Metres   15

blocks, consists of a simple rectangular nave and a smaller square-ended chancel. The nave has windows in its south wall only and is entered through an original doorway which, before the alterations of 1734, stood approximately midway along the south side. The chancel is lit by two original windows in the north and south walls–, slits with wide internal splays. The east gable is windowless. In the south wall of the chancel is the doorway through which the priest would have entered. This was enlarged and embellished in the 15th century.

Internally, the church is unadorned, save for the magnificent 12th-century archway which opens from the nave into the chancel. This is of two orders, the inner supported on massive semi-cylindrical shafts rising from simply-moulded plinths to plain, cushion-headed capitals. The basin of the font, a massive hemisphere with planed-off faces which produces a 'cushion-capital' effect below an octagonal rim, is contemporary with the building.

Aerial photography has revealed the crop-mark remains of an extensive complex of structures on the slopes to the southeast of the church. These may be associated with a 12th-century episcopal residence, an earlier Celtic monastery – a bronze bell of Celtic type is preserved in the church – or a Pictish settlement from which the Class I symbol stone by the churchyard gate may have come (see above).

3.   Drainie
   *c.*NJ 20 69 (Lost)
The fine late-gothic church of Drainie, built in 1666 to serve the united medieval parishes of Kinneddar and Ogstoun, was demolished after World War II to allow an extension to the runway at RAF Lossiemouth.

4.   Dundurcas
   NJ 303 510
On the gravel terrace of the Spey at Kirkhill, 2 miles north of Rothes on the B9015 is the roofless, but otherwise complete, ruin of a plain rectangular church, with a fine bellcot on the west gable. First recorded in the 13th century, most of the

present building is the product of post-Reformation rebuilding but apparently on the medieval foundations. The last major reconstruction is marked by a carved lintel dated 1740.

5. Elgin Cathedral and Chanonry*
NJ 221 630

At the east end of Elgin, signposted north off the A96. Without doubt this was the most beautiful of Scotland's medieval cathedrals, its magnificent ruin mute testimony to the splendour which has gone. The ruins comprise three main portions: the western towers, the south transept, the eastern limb and adjoining chapter-house. In addition, around the church can be traced remains of the medieval precinct wall of the chanonry, with one gate surviving, plus the substantial ruins of one of the canons' manses.

The west front of the cathedral is one of the most impos-ing medieval facades in Scotland. The buttressed towers, each 27.4m high and originally capped by lead-sheathed tim-ber spires, are 13th-century. Between them is the great west door, crowned by triple gablets and contained within a richly carved recessed ingo. The inner division of the doorway is a late 14th- or early 15th-century insertion, luxuriantly carved with vines, oak leaves, acorns and branches. The pointed oval panel above the doors – called a vesica – contained a carving of the Holy Trinity to whom the cathedral was dedicated, and kneeling on either side of this are angels swinging incense-burners. Above the doorway the gable is filled by a large early 15th-century window, its tracery gone, which replaced a group of tall 13th-century lancets. Over the window is a para-pet walkway between the towers, the apex of the gable rising above it. Below the parapet are three coats of arms: on the right are those of the bishopric of Moray; in the centre are the royal arms of Scotland; on the left are the personal arms of Bishop Columba Dunbar (1422–36) who completed the re-building of the gable. The interior wall (up to sill height of the western window) was refaced in the 15th century and carries an arcaded gallery between the towers below the level of the window.

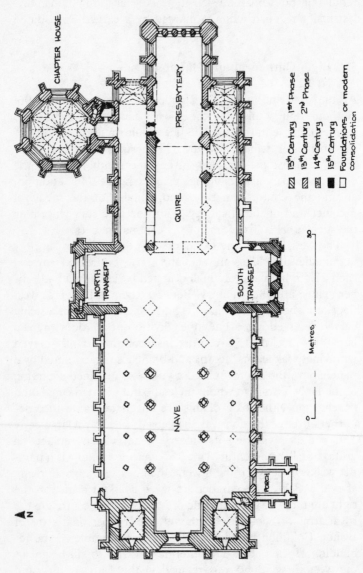

Figure 6. Elgin Cathedral

Most of the nave between the western towers and the crossing has been reduced to low walls and foundations, with only a substantial section of the south wall of the aisle remaining. The nave was of six bays, originally with single aisles, but in the later 13th century the old north and south walls were removed, a second arcade of six bays inserted and new outer walls built 3.15m beyond the former line. As a result of this extension the walls of the aisles project beyond the line of the western towers. The new outer aisles were partitioned by wooden screens into separate chapels, except for the westernmost bay on both sides which contained doorways for public access to the nave. The south doorway survives, its importance as the principal entrance to the church after the ceremonial western processional doorway marked by the outer porch which protected it. This was a substantial chamber with rib-and-panel vaulting and a chamber on the upper floor. The outer wall of the third and fourth bays of the south aisle survives to full height, their late 13th-century windows replaced in the 15th century by large traceried openings. Each bay had a separate gabled roof rather than a continuous roof running the full length of the aisle, an unusual arrangement designed to avoid obstruction of the clerestory windows. The aisles themselves were vaulted with stone, except for the three easternmost bays on the south which had timber ceilings and were the first section to be rebuilt in the late 13th century. Although the piers and superstructure of the nave have vanished, destroyed when the central tower collapsed in 1711, their height can be established from the scars on the eastern wall of the towers. Above the high arches of the nave arcade was the clerestory (there was no blind triforium level) which carried a passage in the thickness of the wall for maintenance access at the upper levels.

There is now a great void where the columns which carried the crossing and lantern tower once stood. There always seems to have been a structural weakness in this part of the building and it was the collapse of the tower which completed the ruin of the cathedral in the early 18th century. Flanking the crossing are the transepts, the oldest portions of the building. These were unaisled structures and originally con-

tained two chapels each. The southern wall of the south transept is relatively complete and is a fine example of early 13th-
century work. The verticality of the four plain buttresses
which divide its face into compartments gives an impression
of greater height, an illusion strengthened by the placing of
shorter round-headed windows in the upper level above tall,
slender lancets, and the steep angle of the surviving portion
of the roof gable above. In the south-west is a fine recessed
doorway with a vesica-shaped window above, provided with
window seats, indicating that there was some form of timber
chamber built into the angle of the transept. The north transept followed a similar layout to the south, except that a stair
rose in a turret in its north-west angle, providing access to the
mural galleries at clerestorey level and to the stairs leading to
the upper levels of the central tower. In both transepts are the
remains of fine tomb recesses: in the south transept those of
Bishop James Stewart (1460–62) into which has been put the
armoured effigy of Robert Innes of Invermarkie whose free-
standing tomb further to the north in the transept has been
destroyed, and the tomb of an unidentified individual; in the
north transept two effigies of members of the Dunbar family
survive, one in 15th-century armour, the other in everyday
dress of an earlier period.

A clear impression of the quality of what has been lost with
the destruction of the nave can be gained from the superb
remains of the eastern limb of the church. This consists of an
aisled quire of four bays and an unaisled presbytery. The
quire began at a stone screen, or *pulpitum*, which stood under
the vanished eastern archway of the crossing. The oak stalls
of the canons began on the back of this and extended along
the north and south walls until approximately the mid-point
of the third bay from the west. On the south side, in front of
the large pier which divides the third and fourth bays, stood
the bishop's throne. This pier projects into the quire at this
point, and its partner on the north side, both rising into
three-tiered spire-like caps, are the dressed up stumps of the
original east gable. The blank masonry of the lower two-
thirds of the north wall belongs to the same building. The
early quire and presbytery thus extended half the length of its

successor and was unaisled. In the later 13th century, after a serious fire, the decision was taken to extend the building eastwards and to provide aisles. The result was the construction of the magnificent east end of the church, with two tiers of lancets and large wheel window in the apex of the gable framed between two octagonal turrets capped by gableted octagonal stone spires. Large traceried windows in both side walls of the presbytery below the magnificently rhythmic lancets of the clerestorey which runs the full length of the east end, added to the blaze of light which must have flooded the area of the high altar, which stood on the highest of the three chancel steps. Under the western of the two south windows is the sedilia, or seats occupied by the clergy officiating at the mass. On the north side of the presbytery is a fine late 13th-century tomb recess, probably belonging to Bishop Archibald (1253–99) who commenced the enlargement of the cathedral after the 1270 fire. A second tomb, believed to be that of Bishop John Pilmore (1326–62), occupied the arcaded opening between the quire and the north aisle, its effigy now placed in the south aisle.

The south aisle of the quire is better preserved than most other portions of the cathedral as a result of it being the burial-place of the Gordons of Huntly. The eastern half is still roofed, its rib-and-panel vaulted ceiling giving a good impression of the now-vanished vaults of the north aisle and the north and south aisles of the nave, while the two eastern windows retain their original tracery. In this aisle are to found some of the best-preserved medieval tomb monuments in Scotland, especially those of Bishop John Winchester (1436–60), the splendid armoured effigy of Sir William de la Hay of Lochloy (d.1422) and the effigy in Chancellor's robes of Alexander Gordon, 1st earl of Huntly (d.1470). The floor is paved with numerous grave-slabs of pre-Reformation clerics. Less survives of the north aisle, of which only the easternmost bay is now vaulted.

Entered through a vestibule opening from the north of the fourth bay of the north quire aisle is the superb English-style octagonal chapter-house. This formed part of the late 13th-century extension but was extensively remodelled in the 15th

century. The entrance vestibule was originally vaulted and in
the 15th century a small chamber, possibly a sacristy, was
built onto its eastern side. The chapter-house itself was reconstructed by Bishop Andrew Stewart (1482–1501), whose
arms appear on the capital of the fine central pillar which carries the sophisticated rib-and-panel vault. The smaller traceried windows were also constructed at this time. The sculpture
of the chapter-house is magnificent, particularly on the corbels and bosses of the vault. On the north wall, opposite the
entrance, are five canopied seats which would have been occupied by the chief dignitaries of the cathedral chapter, while
the lesser canons sat on the plain benches around the other
sides. Immediately to the east of the main doorway is a
smaller doorway opening onto a spiral stair which led to an
upper chamber under the roof. The roof itself is a modern
reconstruction to protect the 15th-century vault from water
damage.

Around the cathedral can still be seen remains of the extensive complex of canons' manses within the precinct wall,
known as the chanonry. The most obvious of these is the
building known as the Bishop's House, across the street to
the north-west. This was probably the Precentor's manse and
is largely of 16th-century date. Before the demolition and collapse of substantial portions of it in the 19th century, it was a
large L-plan house with oriel-windowed hall at first floor level
above vaulted cellars, with stair tower and private accommodation in the wing. To the north of it is North College, the
former Deanery, built in 1520, greatly altered in 1858, and
now a private house. South of the cathedral is South College,
built around the remains of the archdeacon's manse. The
most interesting remains here are of its original enclosure wall
with arched entrance, showing how each manse stood, self-
contained in its private grounds. The whole complex of the
chanonry was enclosed within a precinct wall 3.7m high and
823m long, pierced by four gates. Sections of the wall can
still be seen in the gardens of the housing scheme to the south
of the cathedral, with a fine section containing the only surviving gate, Pan's Port, standing to the east. The archway of
the gate is original, preserving the groove for a portcullis, but

the parapet and battlements are 19th-century, the whole structure having been at least one storey higher with a chamber to house the portcullis lifting mechanism.

Construction of the cathedral may have begun in advance of the transfer of the seat of the bishop from Spynie in 1224 by Bishop Andrew. He, however, was responsible for the building of the first church. This was damaged by a major fire in 1270, the scars of which can still be seen on the stonework of the quire, and the decision was made by Bishop Archibald to extend the building massively rather than simply repair the damage. The result was the structure which we see today. This suffered further extensive damage in 1390 when it was burned on the orders of Alexander Stewart, earl of Buchan and lord of Badenoch, in the course of a long-running and acrimonious dispute with Bishop Alexander Burr (1362–97) and the reconstruction which followed that event was to continue until the late 15th century. In 1402 the chanonry suffered again when it was plundered by the men of Alexander Macdonald, son of Donald, lord of the Isles. With the Reformation of 1560 the cathedral became redundant, Elgin being amply served by St. Giles Kirk, and in 1567 the lead was stripped from its roof by order of the Regent Moray. Despite this, it was still reasonably entire in 1594 when the Catholic earls of Huntly and Erroll attended mass there after their victory over the Protestant earl of Argyll in the Battle of Glenlivet, and the roof timbers survived until 1637 when those of the quire collapsed in a gale. Surprisingly, much of the pre-Reformation furniture was allowed to remain in place, including the rood-screen with its painted depiction of the Crucifixion, but were stripped out and destroyed in 1640 at the instigation of Gilbert Ross, minister of Elgin. Further damage occurred in 1651–8 during the Cromwellian occupation of Scotland. The final blow, however, came on Easter Sunday 1711 when the central tower fell, crushing the nave, whereupon the ruins became a common quarry for the burgh until 1807 when the first steps to preserve the ruins were taken.

6.   Elgin Greyfriars
NJ 219 627

At the east end of Elgin, in enclosed grounds south of
Greyfriars Street. The restored 15th-century church of the
friary of Observantine Franciscans now serves as the chapel
of the adjacent Convent of Mercy which occupies the site of
the medieval cloister. The church is an unaisled, rectangular
structure of uniform height positioned on the north side of
the small cloister. It was well lit, with large windows (the
tracery is 19th-century restoration) in the east and west
gables, four wide windows in the north wall, and a single
window in the east end of the south wall to light the high
altar. The internal division between nave and chancel is
marked externally by two small, pointed-headed windows set
one above the other in the north wall. These lit the rood-loft
and the transverse passage beneath it which led from the
doorway in the south wall into the cloister. A round-headed
doorway in the west end of the north wall provided public
access to the nave.

The interior of the church was quite simple, and its restored form probably gives a fair idea of a late medieval
Franciscan layout. The nave was divided from the chancel by
a screen formed by the passage below the rood loft, which
was supported on corbels in the north and south walls. Two
altars stood against the nave side of the west wall of the
screen and were provided with piscinas for washing the altar-
vessels. There is a stone sink set into the lower of the two
small windows in the north wall, perhaps used as a lavatory
by the friars before entering the chapel for mass. In the east
end there are two aumbries and below the south window is a
recess which probably formed the sedilia, or seat, where the
priest officiating at the mass would sit.

A Franciscan friary was established in Elgin in the 13th
century, but it is believed to have fallen into decline and been
replaced as a new foundation on a fresh site in 1479. Abandoned at the Reformation, the church was preserved as a
courthouse until the mid-17th century, then was used as a
meeting-place for the craft and trade associations of the
burgh before being given as an Episcopalian chapel. It was

abandoned in the 1820s when the new Episcopal church was built in the burgh and stood derelict until restored for the Convent of Mercy.

7. Elgin Maison Dieu
(Lost)

This important medieval hospital lay immediately to the south-east of the burgh, near to the Franciscan friary. Established in the 13th century, it was burned along with the cathedral and the parish church of St. Giles in June 1390 by the men of Alexander Stewart, earl of Buchan, and was subsequently rebuilt. Its ruins are reported to have survived fairly entire until 1750, when they were extensively damaged in a storm. The remains were obliterated in the 19th century by the development of the area as a middle-class suburb.

8. Kincraig
NH 825 048

In a small churchyard beside the old A9, 1 mile south of Kincraig. This chapel, dedicated to St. Drostan, was dependent in the Middle Ages on the parish of Kingussie. The dedication suggests an early origin, but the present structure is apparently of the 16th century. It is a simple rectangular box of undressed rubble with round-arched windows. The doorway in the west wall was replaced in the late 18th century when the chapel was fitted out as a mausoleum.

9. Kingussie Carmelite Friary (Lost)

There are no surviving remains of this obscure house, all trace having been obliterated before the middle of the 18th century. Little is known of its history other than that it was founded by George, earl of Huntly, (d.1501) in his position as lord of Badenoch and that a prior of the house was mentioned in 1565. Despite the continued Catholicism of the Gordons after 1567, the friary seems to have been abandoned swiftly at the Reformation and its buildings plundered for stone.

10. Kinlochlaggan
NN 536 897

The ivy-covered ruins of the late medieval parish church of
St. Kenneth stands on an elevated site overlooking the River
Pattack and the head of Loch Laggan. Much of the existing
walled enclosure appears to be of fairly modern build, but a
recess in the south wall appears to be an original feature.

11. Kinloss Abbey
NJ 065 615

The fragmentary ruins of this once extensive Cistercian
abbey lie largely enclosed within the modern churchyard to
the south of the B9089 through the village. The church has
mainly been reduced to foundations of walls and pier-bases,
which can be traced easily amongst the grave stones. Only
the lower portion of the southern end of the west front
remains, but the south wall, pierced by the footings of the
richly-ornamented eastern processional doorway, can be
followed for its full length. The bases of several of the piers of
the north and south arcades of the nave survive. These are of
bundle-shafted form, indicating a major rebuilding of this
portion of the church towards the end of the 12th century. It
was perhaps at this time that aisles were added for the full
length of the eastern arm of the church, an extremely unusual
arrangement in a Cistercian abbey, but the remains are so
fragmentary as to make dating of this development
impossible. The only substantial portion of the church to
remain is the south transept, which has a groin-vaulted
eastern chapel opening from it.

The cloister is still a clearly-defined enclosure, the inner
wall of the west and south ranges surviving to first floor
height. The scars of the vaulting of the undercroft of the west
range can be seen on the western face of that wall. The south
wall is pierced by the richly-decorated round-arched doorway
of the refectory, re-used as the entrance to a burial vault. Immediately to its east is an arched recess, believed to have
housed a laver, or wash-basin, where the monks washed their
hands before entering the refectory. Projecting from the wall
above these are some surviving corbels which supported the

timber roof of the cloister walk, the line of the roof marked by the horizontal water-table above. Of the east range, only a barrel-vaulted chamber, with a smaller vaulted cell opening from it, survives adjoining the south transept. Above it is a vaulted chamber adjoining the dormitory which occupied the upper floor of the vanished portion of the east range. It is suggested that the vaulted chamber may have housed the abbey's library. The remains of vaulting on the south wall of this surviving portion may indicate the site of the chapter house.

The only other substantial element to survive is the ruin of the abbot's house which stood at the southern end of the east range. It stands outwith the cemetery enclosure, and at the time of writing is swathed in ivy and enclosed by a chainlink fence erected as much to protect it from the unwelcome attention of vandals as to safeguard would-be visitors to its tottering remains. The principal surviving portion is a cylindrical stair tower at the south-east corner of a towerhouse built in the 1530s for Abbot Robert Reid, whose coat-of-arms survives on its south-eastern face. The basement housed vaulted cellars and a kitchen, with a hall on the first floor and private chambers above. Running parallel to the north wall of the interior is a portion of the drain which flushed the latrines, which would have been positioned at the southern end of the dormitory, and which also served the privies in the abbot's house, the garderobe shaft for which is still visible in the thickness of the wall.

The abbey was founded in 1150 by David I and was colonised by monks from Melrose. It attracted considerable early endowments from David and his successors and became one of the largest and wealthiest Cistercian houses in Scotland, with substantial properties in Moray and in Strathisla in Banffshire. Declining standards were tackled in the early 16th century through the efforts of Abbots Thomas Crystall and Robert Reid who developed the monastic library and made provision to have the brethren trained at university, the latter bringing the Italian scholar, Giovanni Ferreri, to educate his monks. The chapter-house continued in use as the parish church for almost a century after the Reformation, until replaced in the 1650s by a new church built at the expense of Alexander Brodie of Lethen. In return, Brodie was given free licence to demolish the abbey buildings for building materials, much being sold to the builders of Cromwell's citadel at Inverness.

12. Kinneddar
NJ 223 696

The walled churchyard lies on the east side of the B9135, 50m south of the main entrance to RAF Lossiemouth. This was an important Christian centre in the 8th century, perhaps the main mission centre for the conversion of the Picts in this area. There was evidently a monastery here of some importance, as evidenced by the fragments of Pictish sculpture from the site (now preserved in Elgin Museum – see above). Its continued importance into the 12th century may be seen in the siting here for a brief period after 1184 of the cathedral of the bishops of Moray. On the relocation of the cathedral to Spynie, Kinneddar reverted to simple parish status and the church was finally abandoned in 1666 when a new building to serve the amalgamated parishes of Kinneddar and Ogstoun was constructed. Apart from some rubbly sections of thick masonry in the north wall of the churchyard, traditionally described as portions of the bishops' castle (see below), the only medieval survival is the slender shaft of the market cross on a stepped plinth at the south end of the burial-ground.

13. Lhanbryde
NJ 271 612

The medieval parish church, described as ruinous and inadequate before its demolition in 1796, stood on an elevated site north of the main road through the village. The last vestiges of the building, a 15th-century tomb recess believed to be that of an Innes of Innes, which appears to have been reset in the 19th century, form the east wall of a burial enclosure in the old kirkyard. It consists of a segmental arch, made up from six straight sections of differing lengths, simply moulded on its outer face, and a mutilated and weathered recumbent effigy of a knight in plate armour. On the north wall of the enclosure is preserved a grave slab dated 1580.

14. Pluscarden Priory
NJ 142 576

Set in a secluded valley, sheltered to the north and west by the high, tree-clad ridge of Heldon Hill, Pluscarden Abbey as it is now known is one of the few functioning monasteries in Scotland, having been recolonised in 1948 from the Benedictine abbey of Prinknash in Gloucestershire. Originally a priory of Valliscaulian monks, an austere order founded in 1205 in the Val des Choux near Dijon in Burgundy, one of only three established in Britain – the others being at Beauly in Inverness-shire and Ardchattan in Argyll – Pluscarden was founded in 1230–31 by Alexander II, possibly in commemoration of his final victory over the MacWilliam family of pretenders to the Scottish crown. By the mid-15th century the original austerity and piety of the monks had faded and the priory had acquired a reputation for laxity and immorality. Unable to correct its own abuses, in 1454 it was merged with Urquhart Priory and its monks admitted to the Benedictine order. Urquhart was thereafter abandoned and the more splendid buildings of Pluscarden housed the merged community. During the Reformation the monastery and its lands passed into the hands of the Setons.

As befitted its status as a royal foundation, Pluscarden was conceived on a monumental scale which dwarfed its two sister houses, but there are suggestions that it was never completed to this grandiose plan: it is possible that the nave rose no higher than the low walls which mark its position today. The nave and transepts are the oldest surviving portion of the church, laid out soon after 1230. Building would seem to have concentrated at first on the crossing and a temporary (wooden?) chapel may have been used by the monks until the presbytery was completed in the third quarter of the 13th century. Both transepts have two eastern chapels with open bays to the chancel, which extends, unaisled, for two more bays. There is no triforium stage, the passage at that level being included in high arched openings which rise to enclose the clerestory windows. Signs of fire-damage in the upper levels are ascribed traditionally (but wrongly) to a burning of the priory by the Wolf of Badenoch in 1390. Traces of medieval painting, including a seated figure of a saint – usually identified as St. John – survive on the transept vaults.

Of the cloister, the east range survived almost entire to be restored in the first stage of re-occupation in the 1940s. It consisted of a large sacristy adjoining the south transept, square chapter-house with ribbed vaulting carried on a single, central column of clustered shafts, a vaulted slype or passage and, at its southern end, a long vaulted chamber of three bays carried on two centrally-positioned pillars which may have served as a refectory. The vaulting of the chapter-house is a 15th-century reconstruction. The upper floor of the range contained the monks' dormitory, and the night stair to the church survives in the south-west angle of the south transept. The prior's house, heavily ruined by the 19th century, stands slightly to the south-east of the southern end of the range. The other buildings around the cloister are modern reconstructions. The whole complex, however, is enclosed within the well-preserved medieval precinct wall, entered through the original gate.

15. St. Mary's Well, Inchberry
NJ 324 553

At St. Mary's, Inchberry near Orton, on the west bank of the Spey, 3.5 miles south of Mosstodloch. Restored in the 19th century, the spring head of St. Mary's Well is a rare survival from the Middle Ages in this part of the country of a water shrine with curative properties, and represents the absorption into Christianity of pagan Celtic traditions of the worship of springs, wells and pools.

16. St. Peter's, Duffus★
NJ 175 686

In the old churchyard, 0.25 miles east of the village of Duffus on the unclassified road to Gordonstoun. Of the 12th-century church established by the Freskin lords of Duffus nothing identifiable now remains. The present roofless structure is largely 18th-century in date, but clearly incorporates much of the late medieval fabric. The main compartment of the building is a simple rectangle, any chancel having been swept away in the 18th-century reconstruction and the east wall rebuilt. The stairs against the east and north walls gave access to timber galleries. The low extension against the west gable, adapted post-Reformation as a burial vault by the Sutherland family, is the surviving base of a 14th-century tower. The projecting, groin-vaulted porch over the south-west doorway of the nave is early 16th-century.

To the south of the church stands the mutilated remains of a medieval market cross, originally of similar form to that at Dallas and Michaelkirk (see below). The chamfered shaft is set into an octagonal, stepped base.

Figure 7. St Peter's Church, Duffus

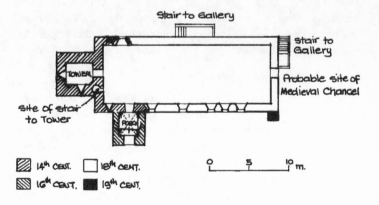

17. Spynie
NJ 228 655

The site of this church, of which the last substantial vestiges disappeared with the collapse of its remaining east gable in the early 19th century, lies in Old Spynie Kirkyard. The position of the now-vanished east end is marked by the floriated head of a medieval wheel cross, set on a 19th-century base.

Spynie was briefly the cathedral of the see of Moray in the early 13th century, following the move from Kinneddar. In 1224 the bishop moved his cathedral to Elgin, and Spynie reverted to simple parish status. The old church was abandoned in the 17th century and a new church built at Quarrywood, 3 miles to the south-west.

18. Urquhart Priory
c.NJ 289 629 (Lost)

The origins of this Benedictine community are obscure, but it appears to have been established as a cell of Dunfermline Abbey in Fife by David I soon after 1125. In 1454 the community merged with that of nearby Pluscarden (see above) and the priory was abandoned in favour of the larger establishment there. The old priory appears to have fallen swiftly into decay and was plundered extensively for building-stone. No remains survive above ground, but there is one large section of carved stone from an arched opening now in Elgin Museum.

Mottes, Castles and Towers

The castle-building tradition in Moray and Badenoch began in the middle of the 12th century with the series of invasions of the region launched under the direction of King David I and his successors. The earliest castles are represented by motte and bailey earthwork fortifications, where a mound of earth formed from the excavated material from an enclosing ditch was heaped up to form an elevated platform on the summit of which was raised a timber tower – the keep – as a residence for the lord and his family. To one side, at a lower level, was an outer enclosure – the bailey – which contained the main domestic buildings, such as barns, stables, workshops, hall etc. In the 12th century, all the structures in the castle would have been of timber.

In most of the examples which survive in this region, the motte stands in isolation without any trace of a bailey, only the massive site of *Duffus Castle* showing the full form. It has been suggested that mottes with baileys are earlier than the stand-alone variety, and Duffus can be dated to the earliest phase of Anglo-Scottish penetration of Moray between 1130 and 1150. Studies of such sites in Ireland and the Welsh Marches, however, have shown that baileys may have been connected with the presence of garrisoning soldiers, used to police a newly-conquered or troublesome territory. Duffus, as the castle of the principal royal tenant imposed on the conquered province, may have served just such a purpose.

Excavations at motte sites elsewhere in Scotland, e.g. at Strachan on Deeside, Roberton in Clydesdale, or Motte of Urr in Galloway, have shown that it was a very long-lived style of defence, continuing in use into the early 14th century. In Moray and Badenoch, some of the simple mottes certainly belong to the later 12th and early 13th-century campaigns against the MacWilliams and their allies. *Bigla Cumming's Castle* near Boat of Garten in Strathspey was probably built in the early 13th century for a son of the earl of Strathearn, and it is possible that the natural gravel mound occupied by the 18th-century barrack building at *Ruthven* near Kingussie (see below p.145) was artificially scarped to form an enormous motte on which the Comyns constructed the caput of their lordship of Badenoch. The large summit area at Ruthven removed any need for an outer bailey, likewise at the royal castle of *Elgin*, where all the buildings appear to have been clustered on the top of the natural (motte-shaped) outcrop.

In the first half of the 13th century there was a move into building in stone and the development of new styles of castle. Large enclosures protected by a stone curtain wall – or *enceinte* – with timber (or stone) buildings ranged round its inner face were now being built by the crown and by some of the greater nobles. The courtyard enclosure built by the

Comyns at Balvenie in Banffshire began its life as such a castle, while *Castle Roy* represents an early building undeveloped in later periods. These were relatively unsophisticated buildings, even if construction in stone represented a significant financial investment, but in the second half of the 13th century they become increasingly elaborate. *Lochindorb*, another Comyn stronghold, has a quadrangular enclosure with projecting towers at its four corners, but with accommodation still provided in timber and stone ranges around the internal courtyard. The most elaborate forms of this type, e.g. Inverlochy in Lochaber and Kildrummy in Strathdon, have accommodation provided in the corner towers. The latest curtain wall castle in this region appears to be represented by the earliest visible phases of the enclosure at *Spynie*, built in the early 14th century by the bishop of Moray to replace a 13th-century residence damaged in the Wars of Independence. Here, the quadrangle appears to have been provided with projecting cylindrical corner towers, the largest, at the south-west, being nearly detached from the outer face of the wall and forming an almost free-standing keep. Even by 14th-century standards, however, this was an old-fashioned layout.

The stability and wealth of the region in the later 13th century also saw the building of less clearly defensive residences by some of the aristocracy. Such buildings are characterised by the so-called hall-house style, where the principal component was a block containing a hall and private accommodation, with out-buildings grouped around it, but with little defensive provision other than a light enclosing palisade. The best-preserved example in northern Scotland is at Rait, near Nairn, but the bleak cliff-like wall at *Rothes*, may represent the fragmentary remains of such a residence. The stone castle built onto the motte and bailey site at Duffus has some hall-house features in the keep which crowned the mound. This was constructed by Reginald Cheyne, probably in the early 14th century at a time when Moray can hardly be said to have been peaceful. Its motte-top site, however, and the replacement of the old timber defences of the bailey with a substantial stone curtain wall, made it more of a fortress than its counterparts such as Rait. It is probable that hall-houses were more common than they now seem, many having been obliterated in later developments. It is also probable that many more were constructed in timber than in stone in a region which seems to have had a relatively abundant supply of wood, and it should be remembered that even relatively important families such as the Gordons of Huntly still lived in wooden residences into the second half of the 15th century.

The freer form of the hall-house may be represented, too, in the castle built at *Darnaway* in the late 14th century for the Dunbar earls of Moray. Here, the timber-roofed great hall appears to have formed an originally free-standing structure to which towers were later added. Alterations in the later Middle Ages and complete rebuilding in the early 19th century, however, have obliterated all indication of the other components of the 14th-century complex.

By the later 14th century the tower-house, the style of structure which was to dominate Scottish castle-building into the 17th century, was already gaining in popularity. It used to be the view that these great vertical blocks of masonry represented a backward step from the sophisticated layouts of the later 13th century, a return to strictly defensive considerations in planning and construction brought about by the severe psychological impact on the Scottish nobility caused by the Wars of Independence. Certainly, these stacks of rooms piled one on top of the other appear to give little concession to comfort, and their apparent isolation from other buildings adds to the air of starkness and utility. Excavations at important early tower-houses, such as Threave in Galloway, have shown, however, that this impression of isolation is a false one and that when originally built the tower formed just the most substantial component of an extensive complex of buildings. Indeed, contrary to the view that the tower formed the main accommodation for the entire household, it is clear that it was normally reserved as the private suite of chambers for the lord and his immediate family. Servants and other dependants lived in the outer buildings clustered within the courtyard which lay at the foot of the tower. At *Spynie*, although the tower-house is a 15th-century insertion into a

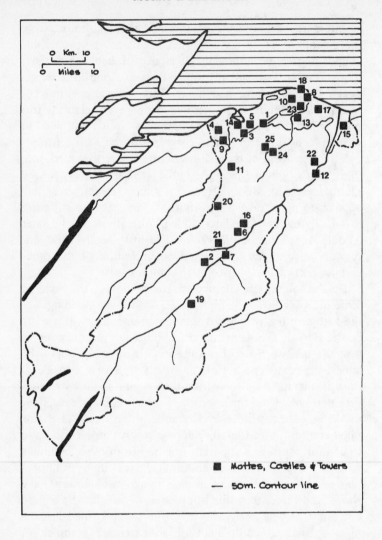

6. The Middle Ages – mottes, castles and towers

14th-century layout, this arrangement of tower serving as private suite for the castle's lord, while the main domestic buildings and service accommodation were ranged around the courtyard enclosure, can be seen clearly in the surviving structure. At late 16th-century *Muckrach*, the remains of a similar layout can be traced. Elsewhere, as for example at *Burgie*, all trace of outbuildings has been swept away. At many humbler towers, it is probable that the outbuildings and enclosing wall – or barmkin – were of light, or timber, construction.

The popularity and longevity of the tower-house form is easy to explain. While some towers were highly sophisticated, as for example those built for King David II at Edinburgh Castle (now fossilised inside the great Half Moon Battery), or for his nephew, Robert II, at Dundonald in Ayrshire, the basic plan and manner of construction was very simple, required little expertise, and they could be built very rapidly. Developments to the simple tower plan removed some of the inconveniences of life in what was, after all, merely an up-ended suite of rooms with minimal privacy. The earliest towers – and the most basic form of plan which was to survive into the 17th century – were simple rectangular blocks. The entrance was often at 1st floor level, reached by a ladder or timber stair from the courtyard, while access to the upper floors was by a staircase built into the thickness of the wall. The basement generally comprised cellars, often roofed with a stone barrel-vault, with a hall and bed-chambers in the upper floors.

The basic rectangular plan put restrictions on the possible internal layout of all but the largest towers. Where the walls were massively thick, the stair could be built into one of the corners, and small chambers – latrines, closets, bed-chambers – put in the thickness of the outer wall. The most impressive tower in the region covered by this book – and the largest built in Scotland – is Bishop David Stewart's massive mid-15th century addition to his palace at Spynie. This is basically rectangular, but the walls are honeycombed with small chambers which served as private rooms opening off the main public areas of the tower-house. In smaller towers there

was less scope for this development and instead the shape of
the building was altered by the addition of a wing – or jamb –
in some early examples large enough only to contain the spiral staircase, but more commonly providing a series of small
chambers, producing an L-shaped layout. The L-plan also
has an improved defensive quality, for the doorway, usually
now at ground-floor level, was placed in the angle between
the main block and the jamb where it could be protected by
loopholes which provided flanking fire across the face of the
walls.

Further refinements of plan saw the stair being squeezed
out of the jamb, which was given over increasingly to private
accommodation, into a separate stair-turret built into the angle between the main block and the wing. These normally
rose from 1st floor level only. There is an excellent example
to be seen at Burgie, while at Muckrach, which was a simple
rectangle in plan at ground level, the stair is corbelled out
from one of the angles of the main tower. Although simple
plans like Muckrach persisted into the late 16th century, after
1500 the building plans became increasingly sophisticated as
attempts were made to fit more accommodation into the basic tower concept. This saw the development of a stepped
plan, or Z-plan, where towers were added as wings to the
main block at diagonally opposite corners of the main block.
This was the original form of the late 16th-century towers at
Blervie, Brodie, Burgie and *Gordon,* but in all these examples
the buildings have been heavily altered or largely demolished.

In most early towers, the main provision for defence was at
the wall-head, where there was normally a parapet walk carried out on corbels, and built out into projecting roundels at
the angles to allow for defensive fire across the face of the
wall. Excellent examples of these survive at Burgie. Most of
the defence otherwise depended on the massive nature of the
building, with large windows only provided in the upper storeys – usually protected by iron grilles (again surviving at
Burgie) – with slit windows in the lower floors. With the development of firearms in the later Middle Ages, the towers
began to be provided with loops for defence by handguns,
usually inserted in the walls of the lower floors. At Spynie,

massive horizontal loops for mounted guns were inserted in the basement of Bishop David's tower and in the Chapel Tower in the mid 16th century.

Firearms, however, gradually rendered the defences of the tower-houses less and less impregnable to well-armed attackers. They were, however, still well-suited to defence against raiding parties, and in the feuds which scarred Moray and Badenoch in the 16th century were to come into their own. Nevertheless, in the more settled areas of the kingdom, the defensive aspect of the tower was gradually overtaken by the domestic side, and while the tower remained the basic form of residence of noblemen of all grades, it was progressively transformed into more of a lightly fortified house than a fortress.

1. **Asliesk Castle**
    NJ 108 597

At Asliesk farm, 0.5 miles east of Brodieshill, south off the A96. The fragmentary remains of the castle stand behind buildings on the north side of the farm. Reduced chiefly to low walls and overgrown mounds of rubble, the ruins are dominated by the substantial standing remains of its northwest angle. Asliesk was an L-plan towerhouse of the 16th or 17th century, with hall on the first floor and stair in a turret corbelled out from the first floor in the re-entrant angle between the main block and the jam. It was formerly a Brodie property.

2. **Bigla Cumming's Castle, Boat of Garten**
    NH 948 197

On the crest of a long gravel ridge on the west bank of the Spey, between the river and the course of the old railway line, to the east of Milton Farm immediately north of Boat of Garten, are the rectangular earthwork remains of the probable centre of the lordship of Glencharnie. The short north and south sides, and long west side, are defended by a broad ditch, still over 2m deep in places, but the west side has been heavily eroded by the river. There are traces of a possible rampart at the north-west angle and along the west

side, where a depression may mark the position of the
entrance. There are no indications of internal structures.

A substantial lordship in this area – of uncertain extent –
was granted by William the Lion before 1185 to Gilbert, earl
of Strathearn. Before 1207 Gilbert granted Glencharnie and
Kinveachy to his younger son, Gilchrist, with whose descendants it remained until the later 14th century. This earthwork was probably built for Gilchrist in the early 13th century.

3. Blervie Castle
   NJ 070 571

Standing like some giant chessman among the farm-buildings
constructed in 1776 with stone from the castle, the north-
west tower of Blervie is the chief survival of a large Z-plan
fortress of the Dunbar family. The tower, attached to the
stump of the main block, rises sheer through five storeys to
the decorative corbel course below the now vanished parapet.
It was vaulted on the first, second and fourth floors. The
tower chambers, which provided private accommodation,
were reached by stairs in a round turret corbelled out from
the first floor in the north-east re-entrant angle between the
tower and the hall. Each room was provided with large
mullioned windows, which represent a later alteration. The
chief survival of the main block is the hall fireplace at first
floor level, bearing the date 1589 on its lintel.

The lands of Blervie are on record by 1238, when they
formed part of the property assigned to the grieve of the royal
castle at Forres. Blervie passed into the hands of the
Dunbars, with whom it remained until the 18th century.

4. Brodie Castle
   NH 979 577

Signposted from the A96 3 miles west of Forres. Although
there has been a castle on this site since at least the 13th
century, the earliest surviving masonry belongs to a fine Z-
plan towerhouse constructed in the years after 1567 by
Alexander Brodie, the twelfth laird. It consisted of a
rectangular main block running roughly north-south, with

large square towers at the south-west and north-east angles. The south-west tower forms the most prominent feature of the south facade of the present, enlarged, structure. The tower rises through a basement and three storeys to an open parapet over a richly moulded band of corbelling, enclosing a gabled and dormered garret chamber. The basement of the tower is a vaulted guard-chamber with slit windows and gunloops, while the rooms above have been designed with greater comfort in mind. The first-floor chamber, now converted into the 'Blue Sitting-Room', was the laird's private chamber entered from the great hall which occupied the entire first floor of the main block (now the Red Drawing Room). The laird's room was also vaulted in stone, now covered by rather crude plasterwork from the 1630s.

In the early 17th century the main body of the castle was doubled in size by construction of a 'wing' which runs parallel to its west front. The old south-west tower thus came to occupy a position mid-way along the widened south front. This extension rises to two storeys and a dormered attic over a vaulted basement. On its first floor, now serving as the Dining Room, was a fashionably new, large room for the laird. In the 1820s a grand scheme of expansion was planned, but fortunately only one wing – the present east wing – was built, running east at right angles to the 1567 main block. Some further internal alterations were undertaken in the 1840s. The grounds of the castle were laid out in a formal manner in the mid-18th century, portions of the original design surviving in the western end of the present avenue and in the pond.

5. Burgie Castle
NJ 093 593

Largely demolished in 1802 to provide stone for the building of Burgie House, the chief survival of the castle is the now free-standing north-west tower of the formerly Z-plan main block. For some bizarre reason the tower was left standing intact and rises sheer through six storeys to the corbelled parapet. The accommodation consists of identical rooms, 4.7m square, floored in wood on every floor except the basement, which has a stone barrel vault. The upper storeys were reached by a staircase carried in a round turret corbelled out from the first floor in the north-east angle between the tower and the main block. The turret has a moulded stringcourse at the level of the parapet corbelling, and widens above that level into a circular caphouse which rises above the level of the battlements. The main tower, and the fragments of the main block projecting from it, are amply provided at basement level with horizontal gunloops. The battlements are carried on a decoratively moulded corbel course, furnished with cannon-shaped waterspouts, and have open rounds at the two northern and the south-western angles.

Of the main block and the south-east tower only grass-grown foundations for the most part remain, except for some jagged fragments against the north-west tower. These show the main block to have been of three storeys and an attic over a vaulted basement, with a high-ceilinged hall at first floor level. The massive fireplace of the hall, its lintel carved with the arms of the castle's Dunbar builders and the date 1602, survives in the inner face of the west wall. A drawing of the castle made in 1799 shows a later 17th-century three-sto-reyed wing running at right angles to the main block from the south-east tower. Some fragments of the enclosing wall of the courtyard on the south side of the castle survive in the later walled garden, and there is an elaborate crow-step gabled doocot to the west of the surviving tower.

The lands of Burgie are first recorded in 1196–7 when they were granted by William the Lion to Kinloss Abbey. They remained a property of the abbey until the Reformation, being made over in 1566 to Alexander Dunbar, Dean of Moray, who may have begun the construction of the castle.

6. Castle Grant
NJ 042 302
In private grounds 1.5 miles north of Grantown-on-Spey stands the forbidding mass of Castle Grant. The core of the present complex structure appears to be a substantial L-plan

tower of *c*.1536, with its square jamb projecting to the south. The main block has crowstep gables, and was presumably originally of vaulted basement, two storeys and an attic. In the angle between the main block and the 16th-century jamb a round stair-turret was corbelled out from first floor level. The jamb was crowned by an open parapet above a decorative band of corbelling and enclosed a cap-house. This original L-plan structure was altered on two occasions in the early 17th century, at which time the cap-house was heightened.

Substantial extensions were undertaken after 1694. The main block was heightened by one storey, its south windows enlarged and regularised and a new doorway cut through in the centre of the wall; an east wing, rising to the same height as the old main block, was built over its east gable, projecting to north and south. The enlarged castle thus appeared symmetrical when viewed from the south, an image enhanced by a second round turret built in the north-east angle to balance the older stair-turret between the main block and jamb of the older work. Both south jambs of the castle were extended south by lower office ranges to form a courtyard area, the space enclosed being made up to form a terrace reached by stairs from the grounds beyond.

In the 1750s a massive classical extension was tacked onto the north front of the castle and the principal line of approach switched to that side. This consisted of a single rectangular block of seven bays and four storeys executed in sombre granite ashlar. It is severely classical, its only concession to decoration being the rusticated quoins of the centrally-placed arched doorway at ground level. The larger rectangular windows on the first and second floors mark the principal apartments of the new building.

The lordship of Freuchie was acquired in *c*.1450 by Duncan Grant, but there is no record of a castle here until 1536. In 1694 Ludovick Grant of Freuchie received a grant of regality over his lordship of Freuchie, and the occasion of this was marked by a change of name of the estate to Castle Grant.

7. **Castle Roy**
    NJ 006 219

Taking its name from the red hue of its stones (Gaelic *Caistel Ruadh*, the Red Castle), the rubble-built quadrangle of Castle Roy squats on a low hillock overlooking the Spey on the northern edge of the village of Nethy Bridge. In plan it is a simple castle of enclosure with plain curtain walls around a courtyard 24m by 15m. Timber buildings would originally have been ranged around the inner faces of the enclosure. The north-west tower, which had a large window in its north face, may have been a later addition. The main gate to the castle was located off-centre in the north wall, the dressed stone of its outer arch long since robbed, but the rougher inner arch surviving.

The castle may have been constructed in its present form soon after 1226 by James, son of Morgrund, earl of Mar, to whom Alexander II had granted the lordship of Abernethy. It is believed that Edward I of England occupied the castle during his triumphant tour round the north of Scotland in autumn 1303.

8. **Caysbrigs**
    NJ 245 673

This enigmatic earthwork stands just off a farm track in an unplanted clearing in dense forestry 2.5 miles south-east of Lossiemouth. It is positioned slightly off the highest ground of an extensive sand and gravel plateau (much of which is being quarried), and is set just back from its south-western edge. Originally, it would have commanded extensive views to the south and west over the marshy ground at the east end of the now drained Spynie Loch. The loch would have added considerably to its defensibility. It forms a sub-circular enclosure, approximately 70m in diameter within a heavily eroded rampart. The rampart, which has been formed from the soil dump of the encircling ditch, stands up to 2.5m high in its better-preserved western section, but has generally slipped into a low mound, in places up to 4m wide. The ditch is heavily silted, but still forms a clearly visible depression *c.*5m wide by 1m deep. There is a single entrance on the south side, where a break in the rampart is approached by a causeway over the ditch. No trace of internal arrangements survive. Without excavation it is impossible to date this site, but it has been suggested that it is a medieval ringwork. It is equally possible, however, that it dates from the Iron Age or earlier.

9. Darnaway Castle
NH 994 550

In 1802 the ancient castle of the earls of Moray was swept away and replaced by the present mock-gothic, pink-sandstone edifice. From old prints of its predecessor, it appears that the new building preserved the T-shaped plan of old Darnaway. Although the fabric of the old castle was removed, the 14th-century timber ceiling of the great hall, known as Randolph's Hall after the Randolph earls of Moray who controlled Darnaway from 1312–46, was preserved. This ceiling is without doubt the finest in Scotland and, until 1987 had been the subject of controversy as to its date. Most arguments favoured a late 15th- or early 16th-century date for its construction, in parallel to the similarly-roofed halls of Edinburgh and Stirling castles, but analysis of the oak timbers used in its construction indicate that it was probably built for John Dunbar, earl of Moray from 1372 to 1392, in about 1387.

10. Duffus Castle*
NJ 189 672

Signposted from the B9012 Elgin to Duffus road, 1.5 miles south of Duffus village. The massive earthwork defences of Duffus Castle, crowned by the tottering ruins of the late-13th-century stone castle, rise boldly from the flatlands of the Laich. Originally a near island in the marshy margins of Spynie Loch, this is unmistakably a fortress of a leading member of the new colonial aristocracy planted in Moray by David I.

The castle consists of two main phases of work with later alterations. The earliest remains are those of the great earth-and-timber motte and bailey, the most impressive in Scotland,

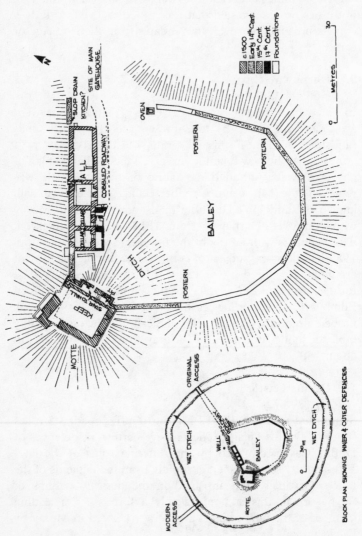

Figure 8. Duffus Castle

constructed in *c*.1150. The truncated cone of the motte, isolated from the bailey by a still formidable ditch, dominates
the site. The bailey, standing on an earthwork plateau to the
east of the motte, is an irregular polygonal enclosure. Enclosing both motte and bailey is a roughly circular outer court,
enclosed by a water-filled ditch. At some stage in the late
13th or early 14th century a massive stone keep was constructed on the summit of the motte, and in a second stage
the bailey was enclosed by a polygonal curtain wall which
survives to almost its full height in places. It has been suggested that the keep was the one recorded as being burned by
the Scots in 1297, but the style of the windows suggests an
early 14th-century date, indicating that this was probably its
successor. It consists of a rectangular main block with a
shallowly-projecting forework which housed the entrance,
stair to the upper floors with pit-prison below it, guard-
chamber with garderobe off it and, on its first floor, a chamber which housed the mechanism for the portcullis. The main
block consisted of a single chamber on each floor, floored
and roofed in timber. The hall was on the first floor, with
private accommodation above. The whole of the keep and
the fine, angled plinth on which it stands, is distorted by subsidence as the motte has slumped under the weight of the
stonework. The entire north-west angle, complete with mural
passage and garderobe, has slid down the face of the mound,
and rests at a 45° angle. The subsidence may have commenced soon after the tower was built, but the drastic collapse may not have occurred until after the building was
unroofed in the 17th century.

In the 15th century the castle was provided with a substantial range of stone buildings along the north wall of the bailey,
including a large hall with adjacent kitchen (its position
marked by a slop drain through the bailey wall) and private
chambers. The whole of this is reduced to foundations. The
gatehouse has disappeared, but its position is indicated by the
line of approach of the stone causeway from the east, leading
from a low stone bridge over the outer ditch. To the south of
the ditch a small medieval bread oven is preserved under
glass. Beam slots in the curtain wall show the former exist-

ence of timber ranges around the east and south sides of the courtyard, while the footings of further stone buildings can be seen to the north of the causeway in the outer bailey.

The lands of Duffus were awarded in *c*.1150 to Freskin the Fleming, whose family adopted the surname of de Moravia, who already held Strabrock in West Lothian from David I. The motte and bailey was complete by 1151 when David I stayed there whilst inspecting building work at Kinloss Abbey. In the 13th century Duffus passed by marriage to the Cheyne family and in 1297 it was held by Sir Reginald Cheyne for Edward I against Andrew Moray and the Scots, who besieged and burned it. It was rebuilt by Sir Reginald and garrisoned for the English occupying forces, but was taken during Robert I's campaign in 1308. In 1452 it was burned by Archibald Douglas, earl of Moray, in the course of the rebellion which followed James II's murder of William, eighth earl of Douglas. Restored again, it was ransacked during the Covenanting wars of the 17th century and abandoned finally in 1705.

11. Dunphail Castle
   NJ 007 481
In the private grounds of Dunphail House, 7 miles south of Forres on the A940. The fragmentary ruin of Dunphail Castle, a property of the Cumming family, occupies a strong defensive position on an isolated rocky mound rising steeply above the east bank of the River Divie and separated from the main slope of the valley. It is believed that there has been a castle on this site since the 13th century, built by a junior branch of the great Comyn/Cumming family. Tradition attributes the destruction of the early castle in 1330 to Thomas Randolph, earl of Moray. The surviving ruin appears to be considerably later, consisting of the remains of a vaulted basement with a two-storeyed gable rising above, each floor provided with large windows in the gable end.

12. Easter Elchies
   NJ 279 444
At the Macallan Distillery, 0.5 miles south on unclassified

road of the B9102 Craigellachie-Archiestown road. This recently restored house of the Grants stands high above the valley of the Spey in a commanding position and can be seen clearly from the A95 south of Craigellachie. It consists of an L-plan tower of two storeys, dormered attic and garret, considerably altered in the 17th and 18th centuries and extended in the 19th. The recent restoration for the Macallan Distillery saw the demolition of the Victorian additions and the construction of a single storey hexagonal wing.

13. Elgin Castle
NJ 211 628

The natural conical mass of Ladyhill, crowned by the monumental column and statue dedicated to the last duke of Richmond and Gordon, is the most prominent feature on the Elgin skyline. A royal castle is believed to have been established here in the reign of David I (1124–53) and certainly by the reign of Malcolm IV (1153–65), who in 1160 granted property in the burgh of Elgin, plus the lands of Innes, to Berowald the Fleming for the service of one knight 'in my castle of Elgin'. In July 1296, Elgin Castle was the most northerly point reached by Edward I of England on his triumphant march through Scotland after his victory over the Scots at Dunbar. Re-taken for the Scots by Andrew Moray in 1297, it was again held for the English until after Robert I's defeat of the Comyns in 1308. Its importance declined thereafter and it appears to have been abandoned and decayed by the 15th century.

Excavation in the early 1970s revealed that the present terraced profile of the hill is the product of post-medieval landscaping, presumably associated with the building of the column and the laying out of a small park in the 19th century, but traces were found of what may have been the footings of a curtain wall part way down the northern slopes. Nothing survived of any curtain-wall enclosing the oval summit, although large quantities of rubble, dressed stones and mortar were uncovered.

The most obvious remnant of the castle is a rectangular structure on the eastern extremity of the summit, its long axis

running north-south, traditionally identified as the Chapel of
Our Lady. The walls are faceless rubble cores, rising to a
maximum height of 1.5m, broken near the north end of the
west side by what appears to have been a doorway. No other
structures were identified during the excavations, and it appears that the summit had been artificially levelled in the
early 19th-century landscaping. A rubbly fragment of what
may have been the curtain wall survives on the southern
slopes, south of the monument.

14. Forres Castle
NJ 034 587

Laid out as a park, little survives of even the earthwork on
which the 12th-century royal castle of Forres was built. It
occupied a natural defensive site above the Mosset Burn at
the west end of the High Street, where the road to Nairn
swung round its northern edge to the bridge over the stream.
Largely plundered for building materials, what remained was
obliterated in the mid-18th century when the site was levelled
for the construction of a house (which was never built). The
castle earthwork can be seen best from the area of park across
the Mosset to the south-west.

15. Gordon Castle
NJ 349 595

In private grounds north of Fochabers off the A96. Three
dislocated sections remain of the massive ducal palace of the
Gordons. The most imposing remnant is the slender six-
storey tower which stood in the centre of the 170m long
south façade of the palace which was developed in 1769 out
of the original late 16th-century Z-plan castle. The detached
east and west wings of the 18th-century mansion survive, the
east as the house of the present owners, the west as offices
and farm buildings. The central tower, although provided
with enlarged windows and with its ground floor
reconstructed as the main entrance porch in 1769, is the sole
remnant of the earlier castle. It formed the south-east tower
of the Z-plan structure. Engravings of this building in the
17th century show it to have been a magnificent Scottish

Renaissance structure, easily outstripping in quality the Gordons' older fortress-palace at Huntly.

The Forest of Enzie was granted by King David II to Sir John Gordon of Strathbogie. Building of the great late medieval fortress was begun by George, 2nd earl of Huntly, soon after 1479, but the magnificent Renaissance palace which grew out of it was largely the work of his great-grandson, George, 4th earl, who was posthumously forfeited by Queen Mary in 1562 after his defeat and death at the battle of Corrichie. His son, also George, was quickly restored to his lands and titles and Gordon Castle reached its pre-1769 peak under his ownership. In 1836 the male line of the Dukes of Gordon died out and the lands and titles passed to the duke of Richmond and Lennox, with whom it remained until 1938 when it was sold to the government in lieu of death duties. Used (and abused) by the army until 1955, when it was bought back by descendants of its former Gordon-Lennox owners, the building had been allowed to deteriorate badly and the decision was taken to raze much of the central block and connecting ranges and adapt the two remaining wings as described above.

16. Grant's Fort, Grantown-on-Spey
NJ 053 316
In forestry on the steep northern slopes of Tomvaich Hill, just under 1.5 miles east-north-east of Castle Grant. This overgrown site was presumably the 12th- or 13th-century caput of the lordship of Freuchie, as Castle Grant was originally known, before its move to the present site in the later Middle Ages.

17. Innes (Knight's Hillock)
NJ 283 651
Overgrown and lying on the edge of a forestry plantation in the grounds of Innes House, 0.5 miles west of Lochhill. The truncated conical earthwork of the motte receives added protection from the fall of ground to the west. It was probably constructed soon after 1160 by Berowald the Fleming, ancestor of the family of Innes, who received the lands of Innes and Nether Urquhart from Malcolm IV.

18. Kinneddar Castle
   NJ 224 696 (lost)

The site of this castle lies on low ground, originally protected on three sides by marshes, in the ploughed field immediately to the north of Kinneddar kirkyard and opposite the main gate of RAF Lossiemouth. It occupied a site of historic importance and became the principal residence of the bishops of Moray from 1184 until their move to Spynie in the early 13th century. Substantial ruins of what appears to have been a polygonal, possibly concentric enclosure around a central keep, were recorded as still standing in the 18th century, but all save a rubbly fragment included in the churchyard wall had disappeared before the middle of the 19th century.

19. Loch an Eilean Castle
   NH 898 089

One of the most frequently-photographed picture-postcard castles in Scotland, Loch an Eilean occupies most of a small island situated near to the eastern shore at the north end of the loch from which it takes its name, 2 miles south of Inverdruie. As it stands it is probably largely of the 15th century, but may occupy the site of the old 'caput' of the lordship of Rothiemurchus. It consists of a ruined square tower, now of two storeys but probably originally of at least three, with a formerly vaulted basement and a hall with fireplace at first floor level. A section of contemporary curtain wall with a gate runs east from the tower's north-east angle. Running south from the tower is a stretch of curtain wall of later build, pierced near its centre by a gateway. Above it on the inner face is a fireplace and a garderobe recess, suggesting that a two-storey range of timber buildings ran south from the tower, but this has been replaced at a later date by a single-storey stone structure. To the south are the remains of a two-storey hall block, earlier than the linking curtain wall, perhaps dating to the early 16th century. The fragmentary remains of a 17th-century east range makes up the fourth side of the quadrangle.

In the early 13th century the lands of Rothiemurchus had

been granted by Alexander II to the bishops of Moray, placing it outwith the control of the Comyn lordship of
Badenoch. Although possession remained with the bishops,
the superiority of the lordship was granted to the Randolph
earls of Moray in 1312, but Bishop Alexander Bur received
recognition from David II that that position had lapsed on
the death of the last earl in 1346. In 1383, in the course of his
long dispute with Alexander Stewart, the Wolf of Badenoch,
Bur leased the lands to Stewart for his lifetime and for the
lifetimes of two successors, and it is possible that the earliest
phase of the building was begun by Stewart. By the later 15th
century the castle was in the hands of the Mackintoshes.

20. Lochindorb Castle
NH 974 363
The castle stands on a natural island about midway along the
bleak sheet of water in the moors of southern Moray from
which it takes its name. In form it is an irregular quadrangle,
its curtain walls some 2.2m thick and standing up to 6.3m
high, occupying almost the full extent of the island. Each

Figure 9. Lochindorb Castle

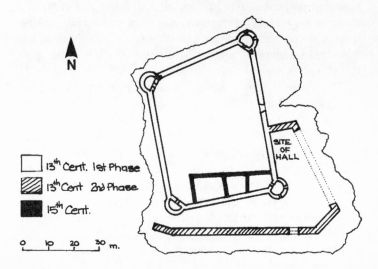

angle was additionally protected by a tower of two storeys and an attic. The two northern towers were almost round, the southern having D-shaped profiles, and in all four the wall to the courtyard was carried across straight with doorways providing access. There are no signs of stairs in the towers, indicating that access to the upper levels and battlements was by ladders. Only the north-east tower survives tolerably entire. Garderobes were inserted in the angle between the wall and the two north and the south-west towers. The towers have small rectangular windows, the north-east and south-west also having long fish-tailed slits of 13th-century type. The principal entrance to this enclosure was in the middle of the north wall, facing the landing-place. A postern gate, now blocked, stood in the west wall.

Outside this enclosure, on the south and east, was a broad area of land which may originally have been defended by a stockade. This, however, was provided with a wall of similar build to the main enclosure, probably soon after the completion of the main structure. In the north-east of this stood a hall, now largely vanished, but the fine, blocked window in its north gable show it to have been a chamber of some pretensions. Near to the east end of the south wall of the outer court are the remains of a gateway, the grooves for a portcullis still visible in its jambs. The interior of both inner and outer enclosures are heavily overgrown with trees and scrub, making it difficult to trace buildings, but against the south wall of the main quadrangle is a range of structures which may be associated with a later phase of building.

The castle is first recorded at the beginning of the 14th century when John II Comyn, lord of Badenoch, died there in c.1303. The structure is, however, considerably older – the fish-tailed arrow-slits in the towers indicate a date in the second half of the 13th century – and was probably built between 1258 and 1275 by John I Comyn of Badenoch as one of the principal fortresses of his lordship. In September 1303 Edward I stayed in the castle. The castle was taken into crown possession on the forfeiture of the Comyn family by Robert I and given by him to his nephew, Thomas Randolph, as part of the great new earldom of Moray. In the civil wars during the minority of David II it came into the possession of David of Strathbogie, earl of Atholl, one of the principal supporters of David's rival, Edward Balliol. After killing Atholl in 1336 at the battle of Culblean, Sir Andrew Moray besieged his widow in the castle, but withdrew in the face of a rescue mission led by Edward III of England. Restored to the Randolphs, it reverted to the crown on the extinction of the male line of the family in 1346 and in 1371 was granted by Robert II to his son, Alexander, to be held by him along with the lordship of Badenoch. Traditionally, it was from Lochindorb that Alexander launched his raid which led to the burning of Forres, Elgin and Pluscarden. By the early 15th century the castle appears to have been in the hands of the Dunbar earls of Moray and passed with the title, by marriage, to Archibald Douglas, younger brother of William, eighth earl of Douglas. During the Douglas rebellion of 1455 it was garrisoned against the crown and was forfeited along with the rest of the Douglases' lands and titles. The castle was seized and dismantled on royal instructions by the Thane of Cawdor, who carried off its iron yett for re-use in his own castle, where it can still be seen. Lochindorb was never subsequently re-occupied.

21. Muckrach Castle
NH 986 250

This castle, restored as a private residence in the 1970s, was constructed in 1598 for Patrick Grant of Rothiemurchus. It stood originally near the south-west angle of a large enclosing barmkin, with outer buildings and offices along its west and east sides. Of these, only the round tower at the south-west angle of the west range still survives in part. The main tower consists of a square central block of three storeys and an attic (the dormers were added in the modern restoration), barrel-vaulted on the ground floor. There is a round stair tower at the north-west angle, corbelled out to the square at its upper level. In the south inner angle of the tower, directly over the entrance, is a round, conical-roofed turret carried on a squinch arch. It is believed that the castle may have been used by the Grants as a dower house.

22. Rothes Castle
NJ 276 489

The fragmentary ruins of this castle, a featureless length of cliff-like wall, cling to lip of steep slopes at the end of a triangular promontory overlooking the town of Rothes. It is suggested that the surviving remains are those of a substantial 13th-century hall-house, built by the de Pollock family who arrived from Renfrewshire as colonists in the later 12th century, which was redeveloped as part of a courtyard castle by the Leslies in the later Middle Ages.

The lands of Rothes came into the possession of the Pollock family, vassals of the Stewarts in Renfrewshire, in the later 12th century, presumably as part of the colonisation of Moray under Malcolm IV and William the Lion. By the 15th century it was in the possession of the Leslies and remained an important stronghold until burned by the Inneses in the 1660s.

23. Spynie Palace*
NJ 230 658

Two miles north of Elgin, signposted off the A941 Elgin-Lossiemouth road. The starkly impressive ruins of the palace of the bishops of Moray stand on the lip of the steep embankment which formed the southern shore of the now drained Spynie Loch. The earliest visible stonework to survive is from the 14th century, but there was an earlier episcopal residence, possibly built in the late 12th century, but certainly there in the 13th century when the bishops moved their seat from Kinneddar to the kirk of Spynie on the crest of the hill 0.25 miles to the south-west (see above). Excavation at the site revealed remains of substantial stone buildings of the early 13th century standing within a ditched enclosure whose outline is followed by the 14th-century enceinte. None of these remains have been left exposed in the consolidation of the site by Historic Scotland.

The great quadrangle of the courtyard, although much altered and rebuilt in the later Middle Ages, follows the line of the 14th-century enclosure. This consisted of a high curtain wall with towers at the two northern and the south-eastern angles. Midway along the south wall was the main gate, blocked in the course of the major reconstruction of the palace in the later 15th century. It ran through a pend beneath a range of buildings against the inner face of the south wall, which included a large chapel at first floor level to the east. This had large pointed windows in the south, reduced in size in the later 15th century but their outlines clearly visible against the blocking stonework. The wide 14th-century windows were replaced by narrower rectangular openings with carved heads and the chapel extended to the west into the space previously occupied by the gate pend. A small aumbry, or wall-cupboard, with a trefoil head, has been inserted in the blocking of the eastern of the surviving windows. The altar stood against a screen at the east end of the chapel, the door

Figure 10. Spynie Palace

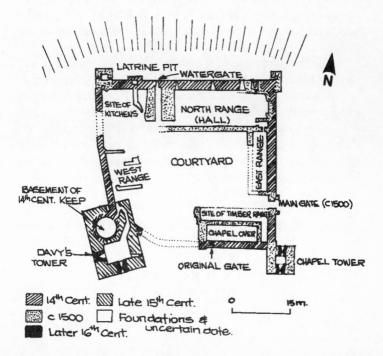

behind it leading into the south-east tower, also rebuilt in the late 15th century and altered in the 16th century, which provided accommodation for the chaplains. The tower, referred to as the Chapel Tower, projects clear of the exteriors of the south and east walls and could provide covering fire along their faces. It rose to three storeys over a vaulted basement, providing comfortable accommodation with fireplaces and privies and was topped by a corbelled parapet with open rounds at the corners. The basement had wide gun-ports inserted in the 16th century to augment its earlier slit windows, that in its north wall covering the 15th-century main gate.

The main feature of the east wall is the splendid new gate built *c.*1500. Designed for show as much as strength, it consisted of an arched opening leading into a pend through the range behind, defended by a portcullis and gates. The portcullis was operated from a chamber over the gate reached by a spiral stair built partly in the thickness of the curtain wall to the north of the passage. Externally, the gate is flanked by two rectangular buttresses which are corbelled out into two angular projections, like ships' prows, which carried the battlements out to give added protective fire along the face of the wall.

Along the north side of the enclosure the ground falls away sharply towards the site of the loch. The whole of this range was rebuilt in *c.*1500 when it became the location of the main public buildings of the palace. At its eastern end was the great hall, entered at courtyard level. It had a timber floor over a deep basement formed by the sharp drop in ground level down the old shore line. There are the remains of a fireplace in the east gable, above which can be seen the steep line of the timber roof which was supported on a row of finely carved corbels along the north wall. There was a privy in the thickness of the wall. To the west of the hall, at basement level, a cobbled passage sloped down under the buildings to the north or Watergate. Beyond that was the bakehouse and kitchens at courtyard level and at the north-west angle the projecting Kitchen Tower, which provided flanking fire along the face of the north wall. This contained accommodation on its three upper floors, possibly for the senior domestic staff of the household. The square profile of its wall-head is a relatively modern restoration and it was probably originally finished with an open parapet carried on machicolations.

Immediately south of the Kitchen Tower the curtain wall has been reduced to its lowest courses and the buildings against its inner face destroyed. The visible remains are those of the 15th- and 16th-century brewhouse. South of the gap, the high stretch of curtain wall is largely 14th-century and contains partly blocked tracery windows at first floor level, possibly those of an original great hall demolished in the late 15th century to accommodate the building of the towerhouse. At the south-west corner the original wall swung round in an arc rather than coming to an angle, and against the outer face of this stood a large cylindrical tower, its foundations preserved under the massive rectangular towerhouse which now occupies the south-west corner. Detached keeps of this sort were rather anachronistic by the 14th century. It is probable that, like the later tower on its site, this one contained the private quarters of the bishops.

The massive towerhouse, known as Davy's Tower after its builder Bishop David Stewart (1461–77), which replaced the 14th-century round tower, dominates the whole site. The largest tower of its kind in Scotland, it rises to five storeys over a vaulted basement, with machicolated parapet enclosing a garret. The entrance is at first floor level in its east side and opened into the bishop's hall. A spiral stair gave access to the upper storeys of private chambers, each provided with closets and privies in the thickness of the wall. In the south front over the large rectangular window which lit the hall, are three armorial panels containing the arms of the bishops of Moray. In the later 16th century Bishop Patrick Hepburn (1538–73) cut massive gun-ports for the use of mounted cannon through the south and west walls of the basement.

Much of the palace as it stands was the work of bishops Andrew de Moravia (1299–1326) and John Pilmore (1326–62), replacing the earlier residence established there by Bishop Bricius Douglas (1203–23). From Bishop Andrew's time Spynie became the chief residence of the bishops of Moray, in place of the older castle at Kinneddar which had been most favoured by his predecessors. The 15th-century redevelopment was begun by David Stewart and completed under his successor, William Tulloch (1477–82). Traditionally, the spur to Stewart's construction of Davy's Tower was threats made by the 1st earl of Huntly, whom he had excommunicated for non-payment of rent. He transformed what had been an old-fashioned, lightly-defended structure into a substantial fortress capable of resisting any but the most determined attacker. During the Reformation Bishop Hepburn took possession of the palace for himself. Queen Mary stayed there in September 1562 on the course of her journey from Inverness to Aberdeen on campaign against the rebellious 4th earl of Huntly, and in 1567 her third husband, James Hepburn, 4th earl of Bothwell, stayed here briefly under the protection of his kinsman the bishop following the abdication of the queen. Seized by the crown after Hepburn's death, James VI granted Spynie to Alexander Lindsay, son of the earl of Crawford, but asked for its return as a residence for the new Protestant bishops of Moray. In 1640 Bishop Guthrie was forced to surrender to the covenanting General Munro and it was subsequently held for the Army of the Covenant by Innes of Innes and Grant of Ballindalloch and besieged in 1645 by the 2nd marquis of Huntly as part of Montrose's Royalist campaign. In 1660 it was restored as an episcopal residence, but after the death of the last bishop there in 1686 it reverted to the crown and was allowed to fall into ruin.

24. Torcastle (Motte)
NJ 129 526

In a field north of the derelict farm-workers' cottages of Torchastle farm, 0.5 miles east of Dallas. The gorse-covered mound of this motte, crowned by a telephone pole, stands part way down the slope of the broad gravel terrace above the flood-plain of the River Lossie less that 0.5 miles south-east of its stone successor (see below). The lands of Dallas were granted by William the Lion to Walter de Rippelay in the late 12th century.

25. Torcastle
NJ 125 530

On a low mound in a field on the south side of the B9010
Elgin to Forres road, immediately west of the junction with
the unclassified road to Dallas, stands a tottering pinnacle of
masonry, the last remains of a late 15th- or 16th-century
towerhouse built by the Cummings of Altyre.

THE POST-MEDIEVAL PERIOD

*c.*1600–*c.*1820

Churches

The Reformation of 1560 represented the beginning of a
long process which was not to be completed until the end of
the 17th century, when the character of the new Protestant
Church of Scotland was finally settled. This was ultimately
Presbyterian, with the focus on the parish and minister,
rather than Episcopalian in the Anglican style which had
been favoured by the crown. The establishment of the new
Church and the revival of spiritual activity at parish level
which was one of its chief objectives, were long, drawn out
processes which the debate over the mode of Church
government served to prolong. The post-Reformation
Church, moreover, was still chronically underfunded.
Despite the disappearance of the monasteries and cathedral
corporations, much of their revenues had found their way
into the hands of the noble families who had managed to
secure control of abbeys as lay administrators before 1560.
As a result, there was little new church-building and in most
cases the medieval buildings were simply refitted to
accommodate the new Presbyterian style of worship. The
emphasis in this was on preaching, not on the sacraments,
and the focus of the church was shifted from the old liturgical
east end where the altar had been sited to the pulpit, which
was often located midway along one of the long walls, usually
on the north.

The medieval buildings were not ideally suited to the new
form of worship. The arrangement of windows, for example,
was designed to illuminate the area of the old altar, while the
main body of the church could be relatively dark. As a result,
the south wall of the old building was often pierced by large
new windows, flooding the new central area around the pulpit with light. Also, whereas the Roman Catholic masses had
physically placed the priest between God and the people, the
minister now stood in the middle of the congregation, which
was ranged in seats around the two end walls and one long

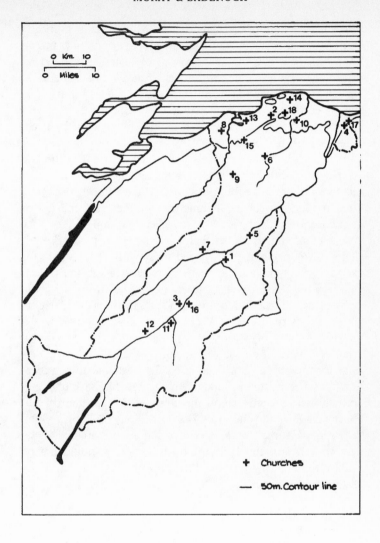

7. The Post-Medieval Period – churches

side. To accommodate the greater numbers attending church, extra space had to be provided in often cramped buildings, resulting in the provision of galleries reached by external staircases. One of the best examples of a medieval church being altered to accommodate the new style of worship – complete with new windows in the south wall and stairs to galleries – can be seen at the ruined church of St. Peter at Duffus (see above p.100).

Many of the early churches continued in use into the late 18th century, but from the late 1600s several had begun to be massively altered or rebuilt in entirety. The church at *Spynie*, built in 1736 re-using materials transported from the site of its medieval predecessor, is an excellent example of the new style of building: spacious, light, T-shaped in plan. The T-shape developed out of the need to provide more space for expanding congregations, an extra gallery facing the pulpit, which was placed centrally in the long wall formed by the cross of the T, was fitted into the 'leg'. In the wealthier parishes, reconstruction of the church in Classical style was a matter of local pride, for the much patched-up medieval buildings were often viewed as unsatisfactorily shabby settings for the proper glorification of God. Such sentiment certainly lay behind the rebuilding of the Muckle Kirk of *Elgin*, and can be detected behind the comments regarding the old church at *Dallas*. While the loss of the old buildings which they replaced must be a matter of regret, the quality of the new churches of the 18th and 19th centuries should not be underestimated or overlooked in an antiquarian devotion for all things more ancient.

1.   Abernethy
NJ 006 218

By the roadside overlooking the Spey 1 mile north of Nethy Bridge on the B970. The present parish kirk was largely built in 1762, but occupies the site of the medieval church dedicated to St. George immediately adjacent to the caput of the medieval lordship of Abernethy at Castle Roy. The 18th-century church was a plain rectangle with round-headed windows, its east wall finished in granite ashlar with the remaining walls of harled rubble. There is a projecting circular bellcote on the south gable. Much of the interior and the additions to the building were carried out in the late 19th century.

2. Alves
NJ 135 636

c.0.5 miles north of Alves village on the unclassified Alves-Burghead road. The pre-Reformation kirk of Alves, reconstructed in 1769-71, stands abandoned in its kirkyard. It is a plain harled rectangle with birdcage bellcote on the east gable and with a series of round-headed windows of varying sizes in its south wall.

3. Alvie
NH 864 094

The parish church and manse stand in isolation on the narrow isthmus between Loch Alvie and Loch Beag, 2.5 miles south of Aviemore. While the church may contain portions of the medieval parish kirk of St. Drostan, the present long rectangular box was built in 1798. The west gable is finished in granite ashlar, but the remaining exterior walls are harled. There are round-headed windows in the south wall and the gables, the west of which has a bellcote, the east a ball finial.

4. Bellie Kirkyard, Fochabers
NJ 353 610

1.25 miles north of Fochabers on the B9104 Fochabers-Spey Bay road. Only fragments survive of the medieval parish kirk of St. Mary and St. Ninian in the old kirkyard. The gravestones and monuments, however, represent a splendid range of types dating from the 16th to 20th centuries. The kirkyard is dominated by the Ionic temple mausoleum to the second wife of the 4th duke of Gordon and their children, built in 1825. A slab dated 1663 marks the grave of William Saunders, first post-Reformation minister of the parish, who died aged 107 after serving his charge for 77 years.

5. Cromdale
NJ 067 289

To the north-west of the village in isolation by the bridge over the Spey. No trace remains of the medieval church of St. Moluag, replaced in 1812 by the present late Georgian granite box with birdcage bellcote, other than an armorial slab commemorating a member of the Grant family and his wife, dated 1602, set over the door in the south wall. The windows in the gables are rectangular, those in the side walls are round-headed. It is possible that the early Celtic church of St. Moluag is represented in the circular enclosure at Congash (see above).

6. Dallas
NJ 122 518

The medieval parish church of St. Michael, described as '*a very ancient fabric, thatched with heath and without windows save two or three narrow slits*', was demolished in 1793 to make way for the present harled rubble Georgian box. The church has a fine doorway with architrave, cornice and Ionic pilasters. To its south stands a late medieval market cross, its chamfered hexagonal shaft set into a massive squared block. The capital terminates in a pinnacle with fleur-de-lis arms.

7. Duthil Kirk and Kirkyard
NH 935 243

On the south side of the A938 at Duthil 5 miles west of Dulnain Bridge. The disused church is a tall, harled late Georgian box built on the site of the medieval parish kirk of St. Peter in 1826. Immediately to its east stands the massive granite ashlar mausoleum of the Grant earls of Seafield, designed in 1837 by William Playfair.

8. Dyke
NH 990 585

On the east side of the main street of the village, 2.5 miles west of Forres by the A96 and unclassified road. This was an important medieval parish with its early origins attested by the fine Class II Pictish stone, known as Rodney's Stone, now preserved in the grounds of Brodie Castle 0.5 miles to the south-west (see above). The present structure was built in 1781 and is an imposing Georgian rectangular box with large round-headed windows and a bellcote on the west gable. Most of the interior fittings of triple-decker pulpit and galleries are original 18th-century.

The churchyard contains several interesting monuments, including the Greek revival vault of the Brodies of Brodie. There is an interesting stone to Walter Kinnaird and his wife Elizabeth Innes, dated 1613. Kinnaird was laird of Culbin, the barony north of Dyke which according to tradition disappeared under the drifting Culbin Sands in 1694.

9. Edinkillie, Dunphail
   NJ 019 465

On a promontory above the gorge of the River Divie on the A940 7.5 miles south of Forres. The present structure replaced its ruinous medieval predecessor in 1741. The main body is a harled cruciform with bellcote on the west gable and porch and vestry crammed into the angles between the long block and the transepts. The windows are rectangular in the side walls, round-headed in the gables and two circular with dressed ashlar quoins. There is a six-sided mort-house of the early 19th century built against the south wall of the churchyard.

10. Elgin
   NJ 216 629

Occupying a central position in the old market area half-way along the High Street. The Muckle Kirk, or medieval church of St. Giles, dominated the heart of the town from the 12th century until 1825 when it was demolished and replaced with the massively austere Grecian revival structure which fills the centre of the street today. Old St. Giles, dilapidated and reduced to only the nave and central tower of a formerly cruciform church, was felt to be inadequate as the burgh kirk of prosperous early 19th-century Elgin. If it had survived only another twenty years it might have undergone restoration, but demolition – which aroused considerable opposition – was felt to be the most viable option. The resulting classical edifice has a massive pillared portico to the west and a tall tower modelled on the monument of Lysicrates at its east end, the whole executed in fine local sandstone ashlar.

11. Insh
NH 835 054
0.25 miles east of Kincraig overlooking the north end of Loch Insh. A pre-Reformation building dedicated to St. Adamnan was replaced in the early 18th century by a plain, long rectangular box. This was expanded into its present form in 1792, with round-headed windows and a birdcage bellcote on the north gable. The only visible reminder of the early Christian origins of this site is a simple bronze bell, dated *c.*900, preserved in a recess in the west wall.

12. Kingussie
NH 761 007
In the churchyard at the east end of the High Street. The medieval parish church of St. Columba was replaced in 1792 by the existing plain harled box with round-headed windows and birdcage bellcote.

13. Kinloss
NJ 064 618
In Kinloss village, on the B9011 Kinloss-Findhorn road. There being no separate pre-Reformation parish kirk, from *c.*1560 until *c.*1650 services were held in the chapterhouse of Kinloss Abbey. As part of his purchase agreement for the abbey buildings, Alexander Brodie of Lethen built a new parish church on the present site. This was replaced in 1765 by the fine T-shaped harled building with imposing hood-moulded square-headed windows. The eastern tower was added in mock Gothic in 1830.

14. Michaelkirk
NJ 194 698
In the grounds of Gordonstoun House, east of Duffus village. At first glance this appears to be a well-preserved late

medieval chapel, but the present structure was built in 1703-5 on the site of the abandoned pre-Reformation parish kirk of Ogstoun. It is constructed in fine 15th-century Gothic style, but the interior is dominated by the massive floor to ceiling provincial Baroque monument to Sir Robert Gordon of Gordonstoun. The finest architectural feature is the west window which fills most of its gable, its superb tracery simple and flowing and with carved flowers in the cusps of the spandrels which link the vertical mullions. Nearby is the late medieval market cross of Ogstoun, its shaft topped by a five-pointed cross finial.

15. Rafford
   NJ 060 562
In the old kirkyard of Rafford on the west side of the village, 1.5 miles south-east of Forres on the B9010 Forres-Elgin road. The fragmentary remains of the old kirk, abandoned and dismantled in 1826 in favour of the new Gillespie Graham gothic sandstone box on the hillside to the north-east, possibly includes portions of the medieval parish church. The west wall is included in a pair of 18th-century burial enclosures, whilst a fragment of the south wall adjoins a burial aisle dated 1640.

16. Rothiemurchus
   NH 886 099
In private grounds off the B970, 1 mile south-west of Inverdruie. The roofless former parish church still stands complete to the wall-head. Built 1827-30 by Thomas Telford and Joseph Mitchell to replace the largely pre-Reformation church of St. Duchaldus, it is not a standard 'Parliamentary church' of the period and incorporates fragments of an earlier building. The west gable is finished with a pedimented birdcage bellcote.

17. St.Ninian's, Tynet
   NJ 378 612
Signposted from the A98, 2.5 miles east of Fochabers. Only the ball finial on the west gable, added in 1799, indicates that

the long, low, unassuming white harled building is more than
just a row of farm cottages. Constructed in 1755, it was the
first building for Catholic worship built in Scotland since the
Reformation, and served the largely Catholic population on
the Gordon lands of the Enzie on the east side of the Spey
estuary. When first built it was still more inconspicuous,
having a thatched roof and unglazed windows, glass and
slates being added in 1799.

18. Spynie (Quarrywood)
NJ 183 643

At Quarrywood, 0.5 miles west of the crossroads with the
B9012 Elgin-Hopeman road, signposted Spynie Church.
This is one of the finest post-Reformation churches in the
region, built in 1736 after the abandonment of the medieval
church site 3 miles to the east. The church stands on a
sloping terrace on the north side of the long Spynie Ridge
and commands fine views across the Laich. It is a T-shaped
structure of long east-west main block and an aisle projecting
to the north, the chief architectural features being in the
south façade. The south-west door is a re-used late medieval
opening salvaged from the old church, as is the superb
bellcote on the west gable. The smaller south-east door has a
flat lintel of 17th-century date, but is also re-used material
from the older church. The dressed stones have been inserted
upside down. Over the door is a small rectangular window
which lights the space under the eastern loft. Symmetrically
placed towards the centre of the south wall are two large
rectangular windows, the blank space between them marking
the position of the pulpit on the interior. Slightly off-centre
between them, just under the eaves, is a sandstone panel
bearing a sundial and the inscription *Johannes Dugall fecit
1736*. The two windows in the east gable light the space
above and below the loft. The adjoining former manse was
rebuilt in 1844 on the site of an older house, whose 16th-
century doocot survives nearby.

Military Roads, Bridges, Barracks and Staging Posts

In the aftermath of the Jacobite Rebellions of 1715 and 1719, the Hanoverian government began to set in place the means for the more effective policing of the Highlands. The appointment of General George Wade as Commander of the Forces in North Britain marked a turning point, for he was keenly aware of the need for improved communications, especially for the provision of roads, to link up the chain of fortified garrison-posts which were to be established at strategic points throughout the region. Over the eight years between 1725 and 1733, Wade's work squads built over 400km of roadway, much of it suitable for wheeled traffic, and around 40 stone bridges in country where previously there had hardly even been rough footpaths and fords were the only means of crossing rivers. Wade's network primarily linked the three forts of the Great Glen and *Ruthven* in Badenoch (see below p.145) with each other, and fed into a road from the south across the Drumochter Pass. This road forked at Dalwhinnie, the western branch crossing to Laggan in Strathspey, then followed the upper reaches of the river to climb via the Corrieyairick Pass to Fort Augustus. The eastern branch passed via Ruthven and Kingussie on the way north to Inverness.

Little survives of Wade's original roads. These have been improved, often later in the 18th century, widened and resurfaced. In many places the road from Drumochter to Inverness has been obliterated by the successive buildings of the A9, and the road from Dalwhinnie to Laggan, while following the line of Wades's road – to be seen especially in the straight stretch which climbs sharply to the north-west of Dalwhinnie – is again mainly modern. The original roads were quite narrow, averaging some 4.8m unless difficult ground forced them to be even narrower, and made few concessions to easy approaches to gradients and the like. One of the finest stretches of the surviving roadway runs from Garvamore to the Corrieyairick, where it ascends the steep hillside in a series of dramatic switchbacks. A second well-preserved stretch runs west from Kinveachy, north of Aviemore, via Sluggan Bridge (see below p.149) to the Slochd Pass, where it rejoins the line of the modern A9.

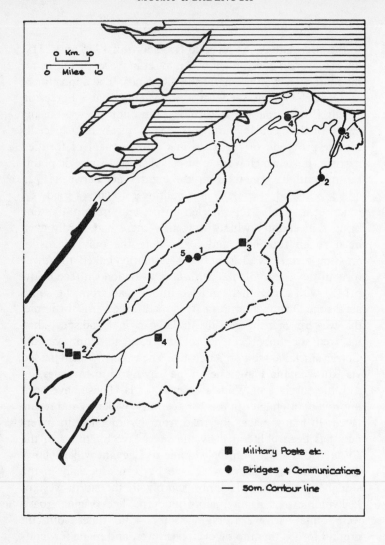

8. The Post-Medieval Period – military posts, bridges and
communications

Many of Wade's bridges were also replaced later in the 18th or 19th centuries, but several good original examples survive in this region. Most were built of undressed stone and were simple, utilitarian structures. The finest of this type to survive is *Garva Bridge*, at the foot of the long ascent towards the Corrieyairick. There is also a good example across the Truim south of Dalwhinnie, where the A889 joins the A9.

A second great road-building phase began in 1740 and continued with interruptions down to 1767. This was carried out under the direction of Wade's former assistant, Major William Caulfield. He was responsible for the construction of the link road from Laggan to Newtonmore, now followed by the line of the A86, and the road from Strathdon via the Lecht to Grantown-on-Spey, and from Grantown across the moors by Lochindorb to Nairn and Fort George. Caulfield's roads were generally better than Wade's, and were laid out with better awareness of the lie of the land. Before 1800 another 1900km of military road and a further 938 bridges had been constructed throughout the Highlands.

To police the Highlands after 1719, new forts and barracks were constructed at strategic centres and older fortifications were provided with new defences. To supervise the territory of the Macphersons and Mackintoshes in Badenoch, and monitor the routes north and west, a major new fort/barracks was constructed on the site of the medieval castle of Ruthven. In addition to these main centres, smaller staging-posts and barracks were constructed at intervals along the road for the convenience of military and civilian road-users. The best-preserved of these is at *Garvamore*, but the old hotel at Dalwhinnie represents a development of the former 'king's house' there. Outwith this region, at Roybridge in Lochaber, there is another well-preserved specimen.

1.   Garva Bridge
NN 521 947

At the head of the unclassified public road from Laggan to Garvamore, 6 miles west of Laggan. Built in 1731-2 to carry General Wade's military road from Dalwhinnie to Fort Augustus across the Spey to the beginning of the long climb to the Corrieyairick Pass, this is possibly the finest surviving Wade bridge in the Highlands. It is 54.9m long, carried over the river on two 12.5m arches with a massively-buttressed central pier, designed to withstand the Spey's fierce spates, resting on a rock in mid-stream.

2.   Garvamore (Kingshouse)
NN 528 943

In an isolated position beside Wade's Road, 5.5 miles west of Laggan and 0.5 miles east of Garva Bridge. This rubble-built structure, also known as Garvamore Barracks, was constructed between 1731 and 1742 as a 'Kingshouse', or inn, to serve military and civilian travellers on the Dalwhinnie-Fort Augustus route. It is a long, two-storeyed structure divided into two main compartments. The east end formed the main inn accommodation, while the west comprised stables on the ground floor and a floored loft with fireplace, possibly for housing troops. The single storey extension to the east and the porches on the south side are later additions. A box bed from the inn is now preserved in the West Highland Museum at Fort William.

3.   Grantown, Old Spey Bridge
NJ 039 264

At Anagach, 0.75 miles south of Grantown-on-Spey, downstream from the present bridge carrying the A95 Grantown to Aberlour road. Built in the second main phase of military road and bridge construction in the Highlands between 1740 and 1767 under the direction of Wade's former assistant Major William Caulfield, the old bridge carried the military road from the Lecht to Nairn and Fort George. Constructed in 1754 by a detachment of men from Lord Charles Hay's Regiment, it comprises three segmental arches increasing in size towards the south. The northern arch was rebuilt following the flood of 1829. The two central piers of the bridge have triangular cut-waters, built out into semi-octagonal refuges at parapet level. The iron railway girders which brace the arches are a modern addition to tie the structure together.

4. Ruthven Barracks*
NN 764 997

On the east side of the Spey opposite Kingussie, signposted down the B970 from the main street of the village. The buildings can be viewed to great advantage from the lay-by on the south-bound carriageway of the A9.

The stark ruins of the Hanoverian barrack, built in 1719-21, occupy the level summit of an isolated gravel hillock rising from the marshy plain of the Spey. Already of great natural strength, the slopes of the mound have been artificially scarped to steepen them further. The main complex of buildings, two barrack blocks of three floors and a garret facing each other across a central courtyard, occupy the eastern end of the mound summit. The barracks are centrally positioned in the north-west and south-east facing walls of the square

Figure 11. Ruthven Barracks

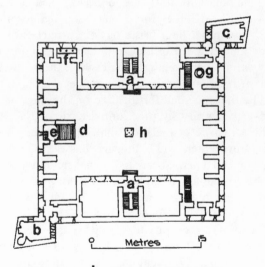

a - Piles of Barracks   b - Brew & Bake-house
c - Guard-house   d - Ramparts Vaulted
e - Officer's Latrines   f - Private-mens' Latrines
g - Draw Well   h - Drain

defensive enclosure, their outer faces being pierced on each floor by musket-loops rather than windows. Each block consisted of six timber-floored rooms, two to a floor, set on either side of a central timber stair. Each room is provided with a fireplace for cooking and heating, and would have contained five double box-beds to accommodate ten men.

The north-east and south-west facing walls carried wallwalks, reached from the courtyard by timber stairs, running over a series of open-ended vaults provided with gun-loops. Originally the enclosure was broken by a single gate placed centrally in the north-east wall, but in 1734 a second gate was cut through the centre of the south-west side to give access to the western end of the mound. There are angle towers of two storeys and a garret at the north and south corners of the enclosure, the northern one having a bakehouse in its ground floor, the southern a guardroom. Latrines were built in the east and west angles.

To the west of the main barrack, reached by the west gate, is a large gabled stable block constructed at the recommendation of General Wade in 1734. It was designed to accommodate the horses for thirty dragoons stationed at the barrack to provide escort duties for military convoys through the district. The upper floor was a hayloft. Stretches of low walling along the perimeter of the mound summit to north and south may simply be retaining walls built in the 18th century, but may be residual remains of the medieval castle of Ruthven.

The first recorded fortification on the site was built in the mid-13th century by the Comyn lords of Badenoch as the principal castle of their lordship, dominating the routes via the Drumochter and Minigaig passes to Atholl and by Laggan and Glen Spean to Lochaber, and complementing the castle at Blair Atholl begun by them in 1269. In 1371 the castle and lordship passed into the hands of Alexander Stewart, the Wolf of Badenoch, third son of King Robert III. In the mid-15th century the castle became a possession of the Gordon earls of Huntly, who largely reconstructed it. Ruinous by the late-17th century, it was acquired by the government in the years after the 1715 Jacobite Rebellion. In 1745 it was successfully defended by a sergeant and twelve men against a besieging Jacobite force of 200, but was forced to surrender to the retreating rebel army the following year and subsequently blown up. It was not reconstructed and is now an Ancient Monument.

Bridges and Communications

Military considerations did not always match with the needs of the local people, and the great network of roads built after 1724 by General Wade and his successors was often unsuited for the growing economic demands of the eastern Highlands, much of it, moreover, having fallen into disrepair as the fear of further Jacobite risings had evaporated. Before 1800 there was no coach service north of the Tay, and it was only in 1806 that a Perth-Inverness service was established. In 1803 the first steps to remedy this situation were taken when the Commission for Highland Roads and Bridges was appointed, it in turn entrusting the physical work of planning an implementation to the great civil engineer, Thomas Telford. Despite government penny-pinching, hostility from local lairds, and the difficulties of geography, by 1820 he had added 1320km of high-quality road and over 1000 new bridges, much of this system forming the basis for the modern network of roads in the Highlands.

1.   Carrbridge
NH 905 229

In Carrbridge, immediately west of the present bridge carrying the B9153 over the River Dulnain. Often wrongly described as a Wade bridge, Carr Bridge was built in 1717 on the orders of Alexander Grant of Castle Grant in response to a petition from the local inhabitants for a safe crossing of the Dulnain for funeral parties going to Duthil kirkyard. The high arch was built to meet the specification that it should be of 'ane reasonable Breadth and Height as will Receive the water when in greatest speat'.

2.   Craigellachie Bridge*
NJ 285 451

0.25 miles west of Craigellachie off the A941 Craigellachie-Rothes road. Thrown across the Spey in a single four-ribbed

45.7m arch of cast-iron, Thomas Telford's engineering masterpiece has withstood the worst that time and the river could throw at it. Springing from abutments of rustic ashlar topped by round castellated turrets, built by Telford's assistant John Simpson, the bridge is carried well clear of the flood level of the river and survived the disastrous spate of 1829 which destroyed, amongst others, Telford's own earlier bridge at Fochabers.

Built between 1812 and 1815 at a cost of £8200 as part of the general development of road and bridge communications in the Highlands under the direction of the Commissioner of Roads and Bridges, it formed a vital bridging-point of the Spey midway between the two main crossings at Grantown and Fochabers. The ironwork was cast at Plas Kynaston in Denbighshire, carried by barge on the Llangollen canal, shipped to the Moray Firth and then brought up the Spey to Craigellachie.

3. Fochabers Bridge
NJ 339 595

Immediately to the south of the modern bridge carrying the A96 over the Spey between Fochabers and Mosstodloch. Completed in 1804 by George Burn, possibly to plans drawn up by Thomas Telford, the bridge replaced the old ferry which had previously offered the lowest crossing point of the river. It was a fine, four-arched structure – two central spans of 30m flanked by two of 23m – with decorative roundels set in the spandrels above each cut-water. In the great flood of 1829 when the river rose 5.5m above its normal level the two western arches were washed away and were replaced by a single wooden span, itself replaced in cast iron in 1852.

At the western end of the bridge is a fine toll-house of c.1830, possibly designed by Archibald Simpson who was responsible for the reconstruction of the bridge after 1829. Doubled in size in recent years, it originally consisted of the southern half only, with three-sided bow facing the river. It is constructed of large blocks of dressed sandstone, its doorway and windows distinguished by bracketed architraves, and wide-eaved roof carried out on decorative ornamental brackets.

4. Newton Toll House
NH 167 631

At the junction of the A96 with the unclassified road to Miltonduff, 2 miles west of Elgin. Built in 1821, the single-storey cottage has something of a fantasy air about it, its plastered stonework painted white, window and door dressings in pale blue and with the window and door architraves picked out in maroon. Architecturally it is hybrid blend of Greek revival (the door is distinguished by its Doric columns) and mock-Tudor (the off-set square stone chimney stacks).

5. Sluggan Bridge
NH 869 220

On the River Dulnain 2.5 miles west of Carrbridge along the unclassified road to Inverlaidnan and Dalnahaitnach. Often described as a Wade Bridge, the fine single arched structure was built following the 1829 floods which carried away a later 18th-century span which had itself replaced the original 18th-century military bridge. Descriptions of the first bridge indicate a lower, two arched structure which restricted the flow of the river with disastrous consequences. In the trees to the west of the bridge can be seen the remains of limekilns in which the lime for the building-mortar was produced.

Industry, Agriculture and Fishing

Moray and Badenoch were – and still are – essentially rural districts with little or no industrial development of any consequence. What early industries there were have left little trace, other than the stone quarries which scar the cliffs between Hopeman and *Covesea*, or which pepper the hillsides in Quarry Wood to the west of Elgin. Ship-building was a thriving industry from the late 18th century at Kingston on the west bank of the Spey estuary, but had gone into terminal decline by the late 19th century and has left virtually no trace in the village. Dunfermline House in Kingston, a largely 18th century structure but possibly incorporating the remains of a fishing-station owned by the monks of nearby Urquhart

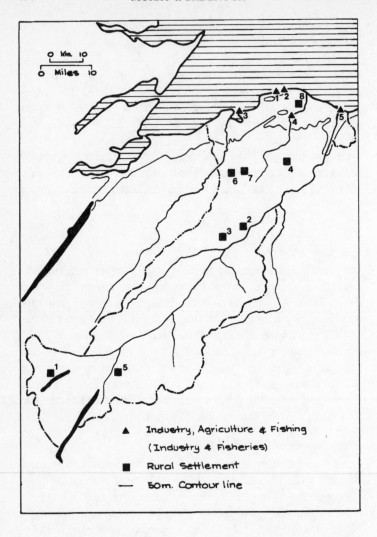

9. The Post-Medieval Period – industry, agriculture and
fishing

Priory, was for a while used as a salmon-curing house and net
store before being expanded in 1780 as the headquarters of
one of the two shipyards in the village.

Kingston, like the other small ports along the Moray coast,
was largely involved in the fishing industry, particularly at
first the lucrative salmon fishery, but later the herring. The
great ice-houses at *Findhorn* and *Tugnet* testify to the importance of the salmon industry to the local economy into the
19th century, but it should be borne in mind that the fisheries
around the mouths of the Findhorn and Spey were major
sources of wealth from at least the 12th century, when they
formed lucrative elements in the properties of the monks of
Kinloss and Urquhart. While Findhorn and Kingston/
Garmouth, and possibly Lossiemouth, are of quite ancient
origin (Findhorn was the port for land-locked Forres),
Burghead and Hopeman are basically 19th-century developments. Hopeman was established in 1805 by William Young
of Inverugie as a fishing village and expanded in the 1830s,
partly in connection with the export of stone from the nearby
Clashach quarries. Burghead, founded in the same year as
Hopeman, was also largely a fishing village, but the large
early 19th-century granaries at the harbour also point to its
former role as an outlet for the agricultural produce of the
Laich.

The agricultural landscape of the region is largely the
product of post-Improvement era of the late 18th and 19th
centuries. Few traces of the older rural patterns can be traced
with certainty in the Moray lowlands, but in Badenoch and in
the hilly districts of southern Moray older settlements, probably of 18th-century date, and clusters of shielings, can be
identified in moorland areas. Particularly fine groups of
shielings, the temporary accommodation used in the summer
month by the herds supervising the dairy stock in their upland grazing areas, can be seen in the corries behind
Aberarder by Loch Laggan and around the lower slopes of
Meall Chuaich, to the east of the A9 north of Dalwhinnie.

The major change to the Moray landscape was the draining of Spynie Loch. The process was begun in the 18th century by a group of local lairds, headed by the Leslies of

Findrassie, whose estates bordered the expanse of marsh and la-
goon which the former coastal inlet had become. A canal was
dug in 1810 to drain the waters into the sea at Lossiemouth,
but it was a further seventy years before the present area of
reclaimed land was finally won from the marshes.

Industry and Fisheries

1. Clashach and Covesea Quarries
   NJ 16 70

Along the cliff faces, 0.5 miles east of Hopeman, by coastal
path from the village, or by access track from the B9040
Hopeman-Lossiemouth road opposite the junction with the
B9012 Hopeman-Duffus road. There are several areas of
substantial quarrying on the cliff faces east of the present
quarry. Immediately east of the current workings is a broad
rubble spill down the steep slopes to the sea and a track
leading round to a series of exposed rock faces scarred by
chisel and wedge marks from the late 18th- and 19th-century,
in front of which can be seen the foundations of a rectangular
building, probably the remains of a cottage. To the west,
behind the cottage site, is a large cave formerly used as a
store. To the east of its entrance there are carvings of a
number of sailing ships. From the quarry the remains of a
track descend to the foreshore, where the ruins of a stone pier
can be traced running across the rock shelves. On its west
side where it runs into the steeper shingle shore is a stone-
built slip-way and about 7m to the west the facing slabs of
what may have been a breakwater or a second pier. 0.25
miles to the east is a second long quarry face, protected from
the sea by a parallel rubble bank. At the east end of the
quarry cut are the remains of a winding staircase which twists
for some 50m to the clifftop, where it joins a trackway built
on a stone causeway which runs westwards to Clashach. At
various places along the shore line rough mill stones can be
seen lying below the tidal margins.

On the headland at the west side of Clashach Cove (NJ
155 704) are the fragmentary remains of a harbour or pier
built in association with the quarries. A broad cartway runs
north along the rim of the old storm beach immediately east

of the golf course and drops into a sunken bed before running out across the shelving rocks of the beach where it was carried on iron shafts, the corroded paired sockets of which can still be followed out to the deeper water beyond. The remains of other structures and landing-stages can be made out in the heath and gorse to the west.

The quarries may be medieval in origin, but their major development dates from the mid-18th century when stone was quarried along a broad stretch of coast from Covesea to Cummingston, which was developed in 1808 as accommodation for the masons. Stone from Clashach was used for the making of millstones, transported by sea along the coast of the Moray Firth. Between 1748 and 1769 the largest customer for Clashach stone was Fort George, where the ramparts are faced in it.

2. Hopeman Icehouse
NJ 145 697

Adjacent to the children's playground on the right at the bottom end of Harbour Street. An early 19th-century tunnel-vaulted chamber for the storage of fish runs south into the steep slope of the old shoreline, immediately to the east of the road viaduct over the track which led to the railhead of the former Burghead to Hopeman railway line. It has a very fine entrance built in the fashion of an Egyptian tomb mouth.

3. Findhorn Icehouse
NJ 036 646

At the north end of the village on the *Salmon Greenie*, between the beach access road and the shore of Findhorn Bay. The salmon fishing on the Findhorn and around its estuary has been a valuable fishery since at least the 12th century when Kinloss Abbey enjoyed the privilege by crown grant. The principal port of Moray until the development of Lossiemouth and the arrival of the railway at Forres, the present village was largely constructed after 1701 when an exceptionally high tide destroyed the sand spit on which the old settlement stood. The village, as well as providing the main through port for Forres and its agricultural hinterland, was an important supplier of salmon and the massive turf-covered stone vaults of the former fish-stores are testimony to the scale of the trade.

4.   Old Mills, Elgin
   NJ 206 630

On the western outskirts of Elgin, down Old Mills road opposite the eastern entrance of Dr. Gray's Hospital. The site of a mill since at least the 13th century (not to be confused with the Bishop's Mill further down the Lossie to the north-east), the present structure belongs largely to a rebuilding in the 1790s, altered by the addition of a substantial kiln with characteristic vent with pyramidal roof at the north end in the 1850s. The main structure is massively built of rubble to bear the weight and vibration of the mill machinery. This was driven by wheels, still in situ, on the east and west walls, powered by water provided by the stone-lined lade channelled from the Lossie. Carried across the lade on arches is a rubble-built granary and cart-shed, provided with a timber-built upper floor.

5.   Tugnet Icehouse
   NJ 348 653

At Spey Bay, 3.75m north of Fochabers on the B9104. The shingle promontory on the east side of the Spey estuary is dominated by the triple hump of the brick barrel vaults of the icehouse rising above an enclosing plinth, built c.1830 in a development of the older fishing station on the site. The structure consists of three vaulted blocks, each divided into two chambers. These would have been packed with ice collected in winter, poured in through doorways high in the curve of the vault. In the floor of each chamber is a sump to allow the draining away of melt-water. Salmon were stored here during netting season before being packed in ice for shipment south. Adjoining the icehouse is an earlier complex, constructed in 1783, comprising a substantial house for the manager/overseer, a large storehouse and a boiling house.

Rural Settlement

1.   Allt a'Chrannaig, Aberarder
NN 492 892

On an elevated site north of the confluence of the Allt a'Chrannaig and the Allt Coire Chrannaig, within an area approximately 200m square, lie the footings of eleven turf-and-stone-built subrectangular and one circular structures, ranging from between 4m x 2m and 2m x 1.2m internally. A second group, consisting of a rectangular ruin, 6.5m x 2.5m within tumbled stone walls, a stone-walled circular structure 3.5m in diameter, four smaller rectangular structures and lengths of enclosing dyke, occupies a spur 200m west. The two groups probably represent seasonally-occupied shielings associated with settlement around Aberarder.

2.   Ballinlagg, Grantown-on-Spey
NJ 06 33

Lying along the lower slopes of the valley of the Allt Breac between Ballinlagg Farm and Knock of Auchnahannet are the remains of an extensive pre-Improvement settlement. Large areas of former cultivation, defined by banks of cleared stones and clearance cairns, lie between the modern road and the burn.

3.   Beinn Mhor, Glen Beg, Grantown-on-Spey
NH 277 997 to NH 282 998

The east and south-eastern slopes of Beinn Mhor, the elongated hump-backed ridge which forms the western side of Glen Beg, have been cultivated at various times over the last four thousand years. The hillside above the 350m contour, on the northern side of the broad, shallow valley which lies south-west of Glenbeg farm, shows evidence of two main phases of cultivation, separated by as much as two thousand years.

Possibly the oldest traces of cultivation are to be seen at the southern edge of a broad triangular terrace which forms a headland jutting eastwards from the main mass of the hill. Here, to be seen most clearly in areas of old heather burning which have stripped away the shallow peat cover, is a scattering of field clearance cairns. The largest concentration, of seven stony mounds measuring between 2m and 3m in diameter, lies close to the bottom of the steeper slopes which rise to the summit of the hill. A second group of three cairns lies some 200m to the south.

The most significant feature of the old agricultural landscape lies around the large Bronze Age cairn at NH 998 277 (see above p.26), and adjacent to the now disused track from Glenbeg to Achnahannet across the bealach between Beinn Mhor and Laggan Hill. About 50m north of the cairn are the stone footings or foundations of two rectangular structures. The larger of the two is a bi-cameral building aligned with its long axis running north-east to south-west parallel to the contours of the hill, measuring 14m by 5m. Approximately 18m to the east are the footings of a smaller rectangular structure, apparently single chambered, measuring 6.5m by 5m. These two structures are outliers of a complex group which uses the burial cairn as its south-west corner. This main group is heavily over grown with broom, but the outline of a large rectilinear enclosure measuring roughly 30m x 50m and containing the rectangular footings of at least five structures, can be traced through this overburden. The cairn has clearly been plundered for stone for the construction of this complex. Outside this enclosure and running parallel to its south-west side (i.e. running up and down hill) are a series of broad rigs, as well as long rickles of stone clearance rather than clearance cairns.

4.   Burn of Red Taingy
NJ 194 502

This isolated site lies at the head of Glen Latterach, 7 miles south of Elgin. Approximately 14m to the east of the abandoned 19th-century crofthouse, and on the same alignment, are the stone footings of what appears to be a longhouse complex, 15m long by 2.5m wide.

5.   Cuaich, Glen Truim
NN 668 885

On the east side of the A9, 1.25 miles north of Cuaich farm.

Behind the deer-fence above the road-cutting, occupying a broad, elongated crescent terrace overlooking the River Truim, are the remains of a dispersed pre-Improvement settlement. The rubble footings of at least three stone-and-turf-built longhouses, together with stretches of enclosing dyke, field-clearance debris, and smaller structures can be traced over an area c.200m long by 100m wide.

6. Little Corshellach, Dallasbraughty
NJ 039 467
Positioned on a slight shelf on south-facing slopes, are the heather-covered footings of a rectangular hut, 6m x 3m. The stone-built walls, 1m wide by c.0.30m high, are broken by a doorway on the south side. Traces of an associated field system can be seen to the north of the adjacent track.

7. Rochuln, Edinkillie
NJ 074 472
The remains of this settlement site stand on a broad ridge overlooking the valley of the Reenlarig Burn. It consists of two rectangular, two-roomed structures, associated with square enclosures and twelve field clearance cairns.

8. Spynie Canal, Spynie
NJ 22 66
Approximately two miles north of Elgin, 0.25 miles beyond the track to Spynie Palace, the A941 crosses the line of the canal, originally cut in 1810 to drain the Spynie Loch. Re-cut in the late 19th century, Spynie Canal still constitutes the main drainage mechanism for the former loch-bed, being fed by a network of smaller channels and canalised water-courses. Despite its initial lack of success, the canal represents one of the most ambitious land-reclamation schemes of the era of Improvement Agriculture.

Mansions and Residences

The trends away from defence in the residences of the greater noblemen which had begun to appear in the late 16th century developed rapidly in the 17th century. Tower-houses

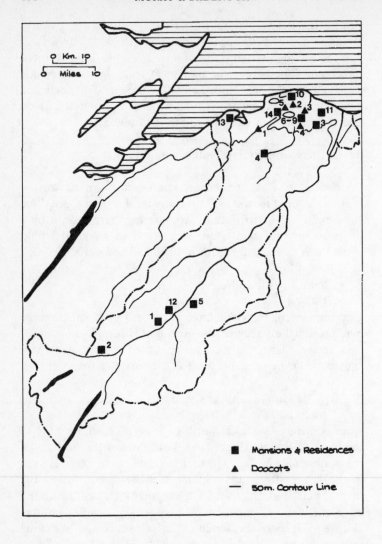

10. The Post-Medieval Period – mansions, residences and
doocots

continued to be built into the first half of the century, indeed, Craigievar in Aberdeenshire, one of the finest of all such castles was completed in 1626, and as the residence of lesser lairds had several decades more of life. One such man, Sir Alexander Innes, still chose to build his new house of *Coxton* in 1644 in the time-honoured tower-house tradition around the same time as his kinsman was commencing the building of *Innes House*. Although Innes is basically a development of the old L-plan form, with a large stair-tower inserted in the re-entrant angle, it makes scarcely any concession to the need for defence, furnished with large windows at even ground-floor level. Essentially, it is a tower-house stripped of all defensive features, such as parapet walks and gunloops, whereas Coxton, with its practically 100% stone construction, looks like the work of a man with a pathological fear of attack. Certainly, Moray in the first half of the 17th century was still not a land entirely at peace. The Moray-Huntly feud had ended only in the 1590s and as recently as 1594 there had been the threat of raids out of the mountainous hinterland following the collapse of Huntly's rebellion of that year. Moray, too, was to be an important battlefield in the Wars of the Covenant against Charles I. Many of the local lairds, including the Inneses, were staunch Covenanters and in 1640 joined General Munro's purge of Royalist strongholds in the north, taking and garrisoning Spynie Palace. In 1645, in the middle of building operations at Innes House, the Royalist army under Montrose campaigned through Moray, and a force under the earl of Huntly besieged Spynie, then held for the Covenant by Innes of Innes and Grant of Ballindalloch.

The greater stability of conditions after 1650 is reflected in the disappearance of fortifications as an important considera-tion in noble house-building even in the more unsettled Highland zone. At Castle Grant (see above p.112) the old L-plan tower-house was remodelled as a comfortable residence, its layout being developed to give a greater degree of Classi-cal symmetry to the irregular outline of the late medieval building. New houses on old sites, such as Grant of Rothiemurchus's work at the *Doune*, dispensed with all last pretence at defence, heralding the arrival of the substantial laird's house tradition where domestic convenience, comfort and the dictates of fashion were paramount. Whereas in the late medieval and renaissance periods the trappings of defence had been part of the social distinctions of the nobility in the houses, by the 18th century Classical purity and architectural austerity had taken over. Older houses were frequently completely remodelled to mask their medieval origins, as at Gordon Castle (see above p.120), or hidden behind 'tasteful' new façades, as at Castle Grant (see above p.112), or the old buildings entirely swept away when the opportunity presented itself, as at *Cluny*. It was only with the growing taste for 'Gothick' architecture in the late 18th century, and the development of the Scots Baronial style in the 19th century, which saw the revival of mock defensive features in the residences of the gentry.

1. Balavil House
NH 791 027

On an elevated site in private grounds, clearly visible from the A9 *c.*2 miles north-east of Kingussie. Built between 1790 and 1796 for James Macpherson, of 'Ossian' fame, to plans by James and Robert Adam, the house began as Belleville and was subsequently Gaelicised in keeping with the Celtic romanticism of its owner. Although altered quite badly in the 19th and early 20th centuries, it retains much of its original classicism.

The entrance is on the north, away from the road, and was an austere composition of harled three-storey main block with dressed ashlar strip quoins and broad bands dividing the floors. It has seven bays with pedimented windows (pediments added 1904-05) on the first floor, the three central bays slightly advanced and surmounted by an ashlar pediment. In the middle of the second floor are the Macpherson arms. The pretentious porch was added in 1899.

The show front is to the south, overlooking the Spey. It was a bold symmetrical arrangement of great sophistication, but has suffered badly in later alterations. Again of seven bays, the eastern and westernmost bays project slightly and carry great Ionic pilasters from the first floor to support a

band of rosetted friezes. The original lines have been ob-
scured by the heightening of attic windows, the addition of
balustraded bay windows to either side of the door, and the
addition of a heavy balustrade over the five central bays, all in
1899. The symmetry was finally broken in 1904-05 by the
construction of a large tower capped by a slated pyramidal
roof against the east gable.

2. Cluny Castle
NN 654 942

Standing high in its wooded policy, overlooking the A86 and
River Spey 1.5 miles east of Laggan, Cluny was built in 1805
to replace the earlier tower of the Cluny Macphersons as a
fine classical villa dressed up to look like a castle. The south
front is the show facade overlooking the valley and is faced in
granite ashlar, while the sides and rear are rubble built. The
central block rises to two storeys over a basement and is
crowned with a corbelled battlement with conical-roofed
bartizans at the corners and on the centre-piece of the south
front. The façade is of three bays, Venetian windows at the
ground floor and three-light on the first; the porch is a late
Victorian addition. Single storey wings to the rear enclose a
small court. The bartizaned north-west wing was added in
1908.

3. Coxton Tower
NJ 261 607

This remarkable tower of three storeys and a basement was
already an anachronism when built in 1644 by Sir Alexander
Innes. A simple rectangle in plan, it is vaulted on all floors
except the topmost, its entrance at first-floor level (originally
reached by a ladder), heavy wrought-iron grilles over most
windows and provided at wall-head level with an open
bartisan on the south angle and conical-roofed round turrets
on the east and west, its builder clearly had defence in mind.

The basement cellar – or cattle-shelter – was accessible by
a door in the middle of its south-east wall, and by a stair from
the first floor. The main stair, serving the upper storeys, rises
in the thickness of the north angle. A second stair in the south

angle rises from the second storey to serve the bartisan at third storey level. There is only one room on each floor.

Figure 12. Coxton Tower

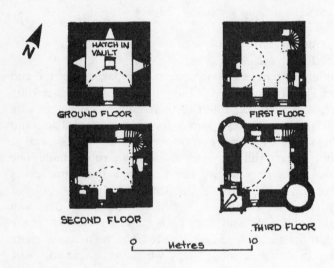

4. Dallas Lodge
NJ 109 527
In private grounds 0.5 miles west of Dallas on the unclassified Dallas-Forres road. Behind the early 20th-century house is the 17th-century 'round square' of two-storeyed, rubble-built and crowstep-gabled domestic buildings, similar to the complete example at Gordonstoun (see below).

5. Doune of Rothiemurchus
NH 886 098
In private grounds on the east side of the Spey, 1.25 miles south of Inverdruie on the B970. The substantial house of the Grants of Rothiemurchus is a complex structure which probably originated in a simple laird's house, now the north

wing. This is rubble built and dates from the late 17th century (heightened to three storeys in 1877). Over the doorway is a lintel carved with the initials PG for Patrick Grant of Rothiemurchus, and the date 1598, believed to have been brought from the family's dower house at Muckrach (see above). This original block was supplemented in the 1780s by a south wing built at right angles to the older house, and from 1797 to 1803 this was heightened and extended to the east to designs by the then owner, Sir John Peter Grant. There is a bow rising the full height of the building to the left of the Georgian main doorway, a Venetian window over the door, and rusticated quoins. A matching wing on the north side of the 17th-century block was never constructed.

The house appears to stand on an ancient site of importance, possibly the early centre of the lordship of Rothiemurchus. It came to the Grants in the 16th century as part of their great extension of landholding through Strathspey. In the early 19th century it was the home of Elizabeth Grant, author of *Memoirs of a Highland Lady*, an important record of Highland life, society and customs at a time of great social upheaval. It contains a memorable account of her home at the Doune.

6. Elgin, Thunderton House
   NJ 215 628

In Thunderton Lane on the south side of the west end of the High Street. The surviving building is but a fragment of the large courtyard house, or *Great Lodging*, used by the Scottish kings when passing through the burgh. It was probably begun in the 14th century to replace the royal castle on Ladyhill and passed successively through the hands of the earls of Moray, Dunbars of Westfield and Sutherlands of Duffus.

At its fullest late-18th-century extent it surrounded a large courtyard and extended south from a broad High Street frontage. The courtyard was dominated by a tall, massively constructed square tower, remodelled by the Sutherlands in the 1650s and demolished in 1822. Engravings of this in the later 18th century show this as a five-storeyed tower, each floor outlined by projecting string-courses, rising to an elaborately corbelled parapet with open rounds at the angles. At its foot was the principal entry to the house from the courtyard standing between two immense caryatids of savages. All that survives, however, are portions of the rear wings of the house, converted into flats and a public house. There are, however, indications of the former quality of the building, particularly on the south side of the surviving range where the wall-head is crowned by four superbly carved pedimented dormers. The north side of this block contains much re-used decorative masonry, including pediments from other dormers. A fountain spout, opening between the fore-legs of two rearing unicorns, is built into the low wall which encloses the small forecourt.

7. Elgin, Braco's Banking House
NJ 219 629

On the north side of the High Street facing the Little Cross, a 1733 replacement of a cross erected in 1402 to mark the entrance to the chanonry round the cathedral. The finest of the surviving late 17th-century houses in Elgin, it was built in 1684 by John Duncan and Margaret Innes as the townhouse of the Inneses of Coxton, their monogrammed initials and the date being carved in the pediments of the dormer windows. Of two storeys and dormered garret, it is distinguished at street level by a squat three-bayed arched arcade rising from squat cylindrical columns under Ionic capitals. The dressed sandstone of the arcade and dormer pediments is contrasted with the rough harling which coats the stonework of the crowstepped gables and upper level of the street front. The house takes its name from William Duff of Braco and Dipple, ancestor of the Duff earls of Fife, who lived there from 1703 to 1722 and ran his banking business from it.

8. Elgin, The Tower
NJ 216 629

On the north side of the High Street opposite the east end of St. Giles' Kirk. The main house, massively altered and Baronialised in 1876, almost submerges the early 17th-century stairtower which projects into the street. The main block was originally of two storeys (heightened to three) with the principal room on the first floor over presumably vaulted cellars at street level. Access to the house was by stair in the surviving circular turret, its top floor corbelled out into a square chamber with crowstep gable to the south. A single pediment from a now blocked dormer survives on its west side. The house was built *c.*1631 for Alexander Leslie, a bailie of the town, whose armorial panel survives in the wall of the tower.

9. Elgin, The Arcades/Red Lion Inn
NJ 217 628

On the south side of the High Street at its east end. No. 42-46 High Street, dated 1688, is the former Red Lion Inn where Johnson and Boswell, on their 1773 tour to the Hebrides, were entertained to 'a vile meal'. It is a substantial three-storey building of five bays with an arcade of five arches carried on squat Ionic columns at street level, the central opening leading through a pend to the inn's back court. No. 50-52 was built in 1694 by the merchant Andrew Ogilvie and his wife Janet Hay, whose initials are carved on the skew-puts of the gables. It is a three-bayed building of three storeys and an attic, its triple arcade carried on squat pillars with Ionic capitals.

10. Gordonstoun
NJ 184 689

In private ground 0.25 miles east of Duffus. At the core of the present Gordonstoun House are the remains of the narrow 16th-century towerhouse of Plewlands. This was a plain rectangular structure with single storey wings to the east and west. In 1616 ponderous two-storeyed wings with squat, cone-roofed corner turrets corbelled out at the angles from the first floor, were added. In 1730 the old fortalice was converted into a classical mansion, and in 1775 given its present flat-roofed profile.

The north façade is carried across flush with the northern face of the flanking wings, which have been refaced and provided with new quoins in the 18th century, and is finished in polished ashlar. The main house is of three floors of eight equal bays with centrally positioned doorway at ground level framed by paired Corinthian columns and pediment. The larger windows of the first floor mark the location of the principal rooms of the 18th-century mansion. The south front, though finished in the same regular arrangement of floors and windows, is rubble-built and incorporates portions of the earlier tower, as is confirmed by the vaulted basement behind it. The wings project beyond the façade of the main block. The wall-head is finished with a stone balustrade enclosing a flat roof, used as a promenade to view the formal gardens and canal to the south. To the south-east are the late 17th-century domestic buildings known as the Round Square, now converted for use as accommodation, library and studies by the School.

Bog of Plewlands, as the estate was formerly known, was acquired by the Gordon earls of Huntly in the 16th century. It remained with the senior line of the family until the 17th century, when it passed to a cadet branch who were responsible for the remodelling of the house and the building of the Michaelkirk (see above). In 1934 the house and grounds were taken over by Dr Kurt Hahn and converted into a private school.

11. Innes House
   ### NJ 278 649

In private grounds north of the unclassified Moss of Meft-Garmouth road, 3.5 miles north-east of Elgin. This wonderful mid-17th-century house is essentially a developed form of the traditional Scottish L-plan tower, with a large square stair-tower inserted in the angle between the main block and the jamb. The L is of three storeys and an attic with pedimented dormers, while the stair-tower is carried up one further storey, accentuating the height of the whole structure, and is finished with a circular cap-house and open balustraded promenade for viewing the grounds. The exterior stonework is harled, but each floor is denoted externally by a projecting stringcourse and each window has a fine carved semi-circular tympanum or triangular pediment carried beyond the face of the rough-cast.

The interior has been substantially altered, but the main arrangement of rooms remains the same with the principal chambers at first floor level. Here was the hall and laird's private chamber, a stair in the thickness of the wall going down to the barrel-vaulted wine cellar below. The upper floors contained bed-chambers and private rooms.

The lands of Innes were granted to Berowald the Fleming in 1160 by Malcolm IV, and remained with his Innes descendants until sold in 1767. An earlier medieval tower was demolished in 1640 to make way for the present structure, which was designed by William Aytoun, responsible for the later stages of work at George Heriot's Hospital in Edinburgh. Work was completed on the new house by 1653, detailed accounts of progress and expenditure being kept by the laird, who appears to have supervised the work personally.

12. Kincraig House
NH 826 064

In private grounds, clearly visible from the A9 6.5 miles north-east of Kingussie. A particularly fine example of a large Highland laird's house of the late 18th century. Its main block is of two storeys and an attic. The central bay of the south front is slightly projecting and the blocking course above the cornice is terminated in two large urn finials. There is a large Venetian window at first floor level of the central bay above the 19th-century porch. On each side of the central block are shallowly projecting single-storeyed wings with Venetian windows in their front gables.

13. Moy House
NJ 016 602

In private grounds but clearly visible from the road, 1.5 miles north-west of Forres on the west side of the Findhorn. This large Georgian mansion was little altered since it was built in 1762 for Sir Ludovic Grant of Grant on the site of an earlier 17th-century house but has recently been gutted in a fire. It is a plainish, three-storeyed house with central one-bayed entrance recessed between two shallowly-projecting two-

bayed wings with heavy, rusticated quoins. The entrance, a
Venetian doorway behind a two-columned Doric portico, is
dignified on its upper level by a large Venetian window.

14. Newton House
NJ 162 635

In private grounds to the west of the B9013 Elgin-Burghead
road, 0.25 miles north of the junction with the A96. The
gutted shell of this fine mansion house, destroyed by fire in
1992, can be glimpsed through the trees and overgrown
rhododendrons of its grounds. At its core is a plain Georgian
classical mansion of two storeys and a dormered attic over a
half-basement, its south façade of five bays with a central
doorway, two wings running north at right-angles to the main
block. This original house, built in 1793, was greatly
extended and 'Baronialised' in 1852 with the addition of
conical roofed corner turrets on the angles of the main block,
a band of false machicolation corbelling at the wall-head with
pedimented dormers rising above, a high tower with oriel
window and stair-turret corbelled out in the angle between it
and the north-east wing and crowstep-gabled caphouse.
There are proposals for its restoration and conversion into
flatted accommodation.

Doocots

1.   Burgie Castle
NJ 093 593

Immediately to the west of the castle ruins (see above p.111).
A well-preserved early 17th-century, lean-to doocot with low
doorway with chamfered jambs positioned midway along its
south front. Over the door is a small window. The doocot is
roofed with small, split-stone slabs, cut through near the
centre by a small projection containing a wooden panel
pierced by four pigeon-holes. There is no ledge on the south
face, but a broad platform formed from thin stone slabs, now
broken away in places, runs from the south-west angle round
the west, north and east sides. In the west gable is a large
opening containing two tiers of three openings for the
pigeons.

2.   Findrassie
NJ 192 654

Standing on private land to the north of the 18th-century house of the Leslies of Findrassie, this fine crow-stepped lectern doocot, dated 1631, is a survivor from the older fortalice on the site.

3.   Lesmurdie
NJ 226 637

In the private grounds of Lesmurdie House, on the north-east edge of Elgin. The house is an 1881 remodelling of an older mansion, of which the early 19th-century doocot is a survivor It is a dressed stone octagon, its angles emphasised by shallowly projecting strapwork quoins. It is divided vertically into three stages, the lower and middle separated by a shallow stringcourse and the middle and upper by a boldly projecting rat-ledge platform onto which open six arched openings for the birds. The roof is a slated octagonal pyramid of shallow pitch, carried out on widely over-sailing eaves.

4.   New Elgin
NJ 221 619

In the park immediately to the east of the Asda superstore. A fine 17th-century circular beehive doocot, rising through three diminishing stages to a flat roof, originally pierced for access by the birds. Each stage is marked by rat-ledges. Internally, it is lined from floor to ceiling with stone-slab nesting boxes.

5.   Quarrywood
NJ 180 642

Standing in a field 100m west of the former manse of Spynie, this large doocot of possibly 16th-century date has been converted in the 19th-century into a water cistern. There is now no entrance at ground level, this presumably having been blocked when it was converted. The side walls are harled, but there are traces of a string-course or rat-ledge about 2m above ground level. Below the eaves level, and running round the crow-stepped gables, is a broad ledge of thin slabs. The roof is covered with large stone slabs, broken at the south-west corner by a small doorway which appears to be a later insertion. In the centre of the roof ridge is a peculiar chimney-like vent.

TOURISM AND TRANSPORT

An Epilogue

The opening up of the central Highlands which the Government's road- and bridge-building policies of the early 1800s fostered received an added boost in the 1840s with the new enthusiasm for the region which Queen Victoria's love of the Highlands fostered. Unlike the Clyde Coast resorts, however, the development of tourism in the central Highlands was predominantly a middle class and aristocratic phenomenon, financially beyond the reach of the large working-class populations of the major towns and cities. Commercial success for this niche market was crowned in 1863 with opening of the railway from Perth to Aviemore, which continued via Grantown-on-Spey to Forres. There it joined the Aberdeen-Inverness line, which had been developed in the late 1850s and 1860s. Until the continuation of the line north from Aviemore via Tomatin and the Strathnairn viaduct to Inverness, the Speyside line was the main route for traffic to the north.

Enthusiasm for the region was maintained through the later Victorian and Edwardian periods, with the vogue for sporting holidays and outdoor activities encouraged by the habits and pastimes of Edward VII and George V. The result of this was the development of large sporting hotels in places such as Nethy Bridge (Nethy Bridge Hotel of 1898-1912) or Grantown-on-Spey (Craiglynne, Ben Mhor, Palace and Grant Arms Hotels), or the construction of major shooting lodges on the sporting estates in the district. Amongst the most striking of these is the massive Ardverikie House (NN 509 876), built for Sir John Ramsden between 1874 and 1879 and incorporating an earlier mansion, which can be seen across Loch Laggan from the A86. This fashion for holidaying in the Highlands led to the development of Aviemore, Nethy Bridge and Newtonmore as holiday resorts between 1863 and 1900, while older settlements such as Grantown-on-Spey and Kingussie underwent rapid development to cater for the expanding tourist market. Here, wealthy

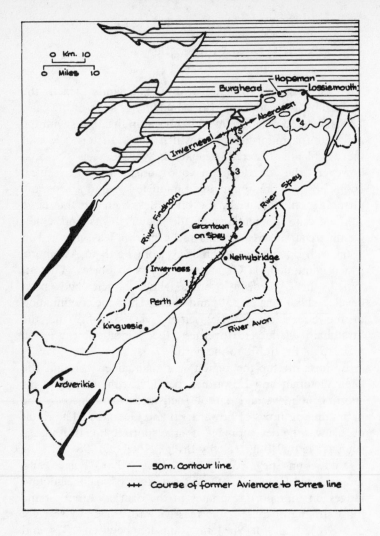

11. Tourism and Transport

middle-class families could build summer villas, or local speculators would build houses for letting during the summer months, a fashion reflected in the large numbers of substantial baronial villas now converted into small hotels or guest houses. Changing fashions and tastes, however, saw this style of holiday enter a long decline after World War I with only a brief resurgence with the growing trend towards motoring holidays in the 1920s and 1930s. Recent years, however, have seen something of a revival.

Lowland Moray offered a wholly different style of holiday and was not so popular with the developing tourist market of the later 19th century. Despite its best efforts, Moray failed to rise to challenge Nairn as a favoured Victorian and Edwardian seaside resort, with only Lossiemouth of the coastal villages receiving investment in the form of large hotels. It was local business which developed mainly, places such as Hopeman and Burghead receiving a major boost by the opening of the railway spur-line from Alves in the late 19th century. This was intended primarily as a goods line, but was popular with the residents of Elgin for summer outings to the seaside. Similar goods lines, intended to carry fish to the southern markets but also bringing tourists to the Moray Firth coast, were developed to Lossiemouth and, via the magnificent metal-trussed railway bridge of 1886, into Banffshire.

1. Aviemore Railway Station
NH 898 129

It is easy now to overlook the railway station in the unlovely sprawl of Aviemore's main street, but this was once the focal point for the village as it grew up in the 1860s. The original 1860s station was replaced in 1898 when the Highland Railway Co. opened its direct line from Aviemore to Inverness, and was, after Inverness itself, the largest of the Company's stations. The buildings are of timber and run north-south along the west platform. The platform is covered by a double-ridged awning supported on cast-iron columns, with bold cast spandrels decorated by wheel motifs supporting the roof brackets. The east platform is roofed by a free-standing awning of the same design, reached by a lattice-girder footbridge.

Opposite the station is the rambling Cairngorm Hotel, built *c.*1900 in association with the opening of the direct route to Inverness. It has magnificently barge-boarded gables and is finished asymmetrically with a round, conically-roofed tower.

2.   Castle Grant East Lodge
   NJ 033 302

On the east side of the A939, adjacent to the railway bridge, 1.5 miles north of Grantown-on-Spey. This superb gate-lodge, which doubled as a private railway station for the Earl of Seafield, was built in 1864 as a gift from the Inverness and Perth Railway Co. to the earl, across whose estate the line from Aviemore to Forres ran. Designed to look like a miniature towerhouse, it was built against the railway embankment as an integral part of the bridge design. It is heavily baronial in style, with a chunky cylindrical tower at its NW angle, from whose upper floor the earl could enter the train.

3.   Edinkillie Railway Viaduct
   NJ 022 464

Like a monumental backdrop to the 18th-century parish church at Edinkillie, the seven-arched viaduct of rusticated sandstone strides across the deep valley of the River Divie. Built between 1861 and 1863 for the Grantown-Forres Highland Railway, it once carried the main line from Perth to Inverness before the cutting of the line from Aviemore to Inverness in the 1890s. It is now redundant.

4.   Elgin Old Station
   NJ 221 212

Replaced by the soulless modern box a few hundred metres along the line to the west, the old station in Elgin was for a number of years used simply as a goods yard until converted for use as offices. The present building, itself a replacement of an earlier station on the same site, was built in 1898 for the

Great North of Scotland Railway Co. It is a splendid piece of late Victorian railway architecture, asymmetrically designed with a western tower, square at its base, then battered into the round and finished with a high, slated cone roof, crowstepped gables, gabled semi-dormers and projecting oriels at first floor level in the two shallowly projecting wings in its south front. Between these two wings is the glass-roofed carriage stance. The interior is remarkably unaltered despite conversion to office use, and is a wonderful example of turn-of-the-century panelling and brass-work.

Opposite the station is the Laich Moray Hotel, designed and built in 1853 as a railway hotel to cater for travellers on the new line. It is a striking piece of English Italianate architecture, its symmetrically-planned south façade looking across the street to the station's main entrance, and would look more at home in suburban London or a south-coast seaside resort.

5. Forres Station
NJ 029 589

Separated from the town by the northern by-pass carrying the A96, Forres Station was once one of the most important junctions in northern Scotland. Here the line from Grantown-on-Spey, from the 1860s until the opening in the late 1890s of the Perth-Aviemore-Inverness line – the main railway connection to the south – joined the Inverness-Aberdeen line. The southern route is now closed, its line now built over by the modern south-western suburbs of the town, and the large Victorian station-buildings largely demolished and replaced by a 1950s utilitarian brick box. The chief survival of the old station, however, is the magnificent glass-roofed canopy which runs along the southern platform of the Aberdeen-Inverness line. The canopy's girders are supported on slender cast-iron pillars, with richly-foliated cast-iron semi-spandrels arching towards the line. The roof ridge is decorated by a continuous motif of cast-iron thistles.

BIBLIOGRAPHY AND FURTHER READING

Close-Brooks, J., *Exploring Scoland's Heritage: The Highlands* (HMSO, 1986)

Fawcett, R., *Scottish Medieval Churches* (HMSO, 1985)

Fawcett, R., *Scottish Abbeys and Priories* (London, 1994)

Gifford, J., *The Buildings of Scotland. Highlands and Islands* (London, 1992)

Hanson, W.S., *Agricola and the Conquest of the North* (London, 1987)

Henshall, A., *The Chambered Tombs of Scotland*, volume 1 (Edinburgh, 1963)

Laing, L. and Laing, J., *The Picts and the Scots* (Stroud, 1993)

McKean, C., *The District of Moray. An Illustrated Architectural Guide* (Edinburgh, 1987)

Omand, D., (ed.), *The Moray Book* (Edinburgh, 1976)

Ritchie, G. and Ritchie, A., *Scotland: Archaeology and Early History* (Edinburgh, 1991)

Sellar, W.D.H., (ed.), *Moray: Province and People* (Scottish Society for Northern Studies, 1993)

Shepherd, I.A.G., *Exploring Scotland's Heritage: Grampian* (HMSO, 1986)

Tabraham, C., *Scottish Castles and Fortifications* (HMSO, 1986)

Wickham-Jones, C.R., *Scotland's First Settlers* (London, 1994)